"There is no bigger issue right now than winning the culture war—and there is no better person to show us how to fight than my friend Kira Davis. This book is a must-read for any American who is sick of the chaos and insanity that seems to have infected every part of our society, but isn't sure what to do about it. If we want sanity and decency to prevail, we can't sit on the sidelines. Everyone must participate and Kira not only shows you how—but how to have fun while doing it!"

—Steve Hilton, Fox News

"A no-holds-barred battle plan for conservatives who are done talking and want to start acting to fix our broken culture and country."

—Dan Bongino, *New York Times* bestselling author and host of the top-ranked podcast *The Dan Bongino Show*

"Kira Davis is one of the most prolific political commentators in America, and she understands the importance of competing on the battlefield of ideas. *Drawing Lines* is a must read for those who are looking to engage in this fight."

—Darvio Morrow, CEO of First Class Broadcasting (FCB)

"My friend Kira Davis gets it in a way the cruise ship conservatives and establishment hacks don't. We're not going to win with the failed tactics of the age of managed decline. We need to take the offensive, and *Drawing Lines* shows you how. The enemy is that way—attack!"

—Kurt Schlichter, author, media host, veteran, and attorney

"I've spent more time discussing conservatives and culture with Kira than with anyone else and I can unequivocally state that there is no one better to examine the topics and issue marching orders (she's brilliant at that). It IS time for conservatives to push back and have fun doing it."

—Stephen Kruiser, comedian/PJ Media senior columnist

DRAWING LINES

Why Conservatives Must Begin
to Battle Fiercely in the Arena of Ideas

BY KIRA DAVIS

FIDELIS
PUBLISHING

FIDELIS PUBLISHING ®

ISBN: 9781737176343
ISBN (eBook): 9781737176350

DRAWING LINES
Why Conservatives Must Begin to Battle Fiercely in the Arena of Ideas

© 2022 Kira Davis

Cover Design by Diana Lawrence
Interior Design by Xcel Graphic
Edited by Amanda Varian

Scripture is taken from: (NIV) New International Version®, NIV® Scripture comes from Holy Bible, Copyright ©1973, 1978, 1984, 2011 by Biblica, Inc.® Used by permission. All rights reserved worldwide.

Order at www.faithfultext.com for a significant discount. Use the contact form from our website to inquire about bulk purchase discounts.

FIDELIS
PUBLISHING

Fidelis Publishing, LLC Sterling, VA • Nashville, TN
www.fidelispublishing.com
Manufactured in the United States of America
10 9 8 7 6 5 4 3 2 1

I dedicate this book to my husband, Mark, who says yes too every crazy idea I have and then keeps everything running while I bring those crazy ideas to life . . . . and to my father-in-law, Victor Davis, my biggest fan and greatest mentor.

Many thanks to my friend and colleague, Katie Pavlich, who made me believe what I had to say was worth sharing, and to Mrs. Zwirecki, a wonderful researcher and an even better friend.

CONTENTS

INTRODUCTION

There is a time for everything, and a season for every activity under heaven: a time to be born and a time to die, a time to plant and a time to uproot, a time to kill and a time to heal, a time to tear down and a time to build, a time to weep and a time to laugh, a time to mourn and a time to dance, a time to scatter stones and a time to gather them, a time to embrace and a time to refrain, a time to search and a time to give up, a time to keep and a time to throw away, a time to tear and a time to mend, a time to be silent and a time to speak, a time to love and a time to hate, a time for war and a time for peace.

—Ecclesiastes 3:1–8

The summer of 2020—which I like to refer to as the Summer O' BLM (the summer of Black Lives Matter)—hit me with a double whammy. Our state and local governments were leaning hard into COVID overreach, and I was disappointed in myself for ever thinking the majority of Americans would choose freedom over government-enforced "safety." The solutions didn't seem to at all match the problem and yet we were hurtling headfirst into all the wrong decisions. This mother's heart was breaking to see my eldest robbed of his senior year of high school, and then his freshman year of college. It all felt like a knife in the back.

Then the knife was twisted. Even as the "lockdown forever" crowd were calling their fellow citizens murderers and granny-killers for wanting to keep their businesses open and kids in school, those same people were cheering on the thousands of protesters pouring into the streets to protest police brutality. It was a slap in the face, and I think it stung more for me because I was being told I was supposed to support the chaos in the streets because I am Black. It made me angry—here I was trying to launch my Black son into his next phase in life, and doing something the protesters kept telling us was nearly impossible for too many Black men . . . we were sending him to college. Instead of being celebrated, he was being tied down. We watched as rioters were treated as "mostly peaceful" heroes, and my son was treated as though he were a walking biological weapon.

I'd had enough. None of this made sense and I was tired of feeling so confused all the time. I'd been calling for peace, for grace, for understanding, but I'd not been calling for action. I realized all these people were getting what they wanted because they were behaving badly. Conservatives like me were standing by, feeling anxious, feeling like things just weren't "fair." We imagined we'd settle it all at the ballot box but that's not what happened either. Things only got worse. I realized the time had come for us to get uncomfortable. We were just as much to blame for the chaos as the rioters and looters. We stood by, pretending we were the "peaceful" ones, when perhaps we were often just being the weak ones. We did not take charge of the direction of our politics the way the left does, and we were paying for it.

That's when I realized there is a time for everything, and perhaps our time had come to get a little bolder, a little louder, a little more insistent.

THE TIME HAS COME

The time for "live and let live" has drawn to a close, at least temporarily.

For too long, right-of-center Americans have been satisfied to leave their voices to the ballot box. They're not interested in constant agitation or protesting. They have an innate distrust of government, and therefore often leave the distasteful job of governing, and monitoring those who govern, to others. The truth is, most people just want to go to work, earn a living, and go home to their families. They expect the people they elected to protect their rights and leave them alone.

Sometimes the political right has been too satisfied to give their voice to a personality. We conservatives like to ridicule our liberal counterparts for being so enamored with the political utterances of celebrities, and so convinced their favorite politicians are good and right and unassailable. We laugh at their naivete and their blind devotion to media and political personalities based on what they wish that person was, rather than who they are in reality. We are deceiving ourselves if we think that is a quality exclusive to the left. We do it too. We trash progressives for lending undue weight to celebrity commentary, but when a celebrity strays into right-wing territory, conservatives go nuts for them. We should be careful not to presume idol-worship is exclusive to an ideology.

Where we were once just locked in an endless go-round with ideological opposites, now we find ourselves on the losing end of a lot of important social issues and pushed out of the mechanisms of choice. The global pandemic stripped us of a lot of the beautiful distractions this country has to offer. Suddenly we are staring at the raw condition of our society, and the image staring back does not reflect the America we thought, or hoped, we were living in. Parents have found themselves at odds with their own school districts. Businesses have found themselves at the mercy of flaky and hypocritical politicians. Our elections process has been thrown into an atmosphere of chaos and distrust. We currently reside under an administration that is failing the American people at every juncture.

Everything seems upside down and no one seems quite sure what to do to set it right.

I have built a brand on reaching out to the other side, on giving people space to be wrong, the space to discuss, the space to tolerate. I sincerely believe there are many reasonable people in America from all ideologies who are still willing to talk with each other, people who are quite happy to live and let live, even if they do find each other more than a bit annoying.

Unfortunately, none of those people are controlling the conversations right now. Trump's presidency has burned away the niceties that tenuously held our political ecosystem together. We've had a front-row seat to the strategy of the progressive left. We're seeing the lengths they will go to and the lies they let stand in service of winning and crushing 50 percent of this nation.

The onslaught of dishonesty has been relentless. The progressive left isn't happy to just let us live with our own values, our own media, our own cultural verticals. They seek unity but only at the cost of the thorough elimination of the other side.

There are times for compromise and times to draw a line in the sand, and friends, the latter has arrived. It is time to draw our lines. Many thought the battle was the election, but that was simply the opening shot fired. The actual battle is unfolding before our very eyes across every single social class and industry.

Progressive-run media entities are deliberately misleading their viewers, covering up information the public deserves to know, and engaging in the type of censorship and malpractice that would have ended their publications and channels fifty years ago.

Hollywood productions and Major League Baseball called for boycotts of Georgia and Texas over their attempts to pass election integrity legislation. Airline companies and Coca-Cola very publicly registered their condemnation. These entities and the people who run them constantly bemoan the "division" in this country even as they willingly make half of their customer base into automatic enemies with every new statement of protest they register. They have made what we eat and drink political. They have made biology political. They have made flying political. They have made our national pastime political.

The election of Donald Trump put windows in the factory and gave us a terrifying glimpse into how the sausage gets made. The ousting of Trump should have closed the shades but instead, it has shed even more light on the ugly process. Now we're not just seeing how the sausage gets made, we're watching the animals be butchered in real-time. It's not pretty, and that means the coming shift change at that factory won't be pretty either.

INSPIRATION

The first part of this introduction is based on a column I wrote for *RedState*, where I have been editor-at-large and now Deputy Managing Editor for the past several years. All the letters and questions I fielded from frustrated listeners and readers were weighing on my heart. I felt it was time for a call to action. I don't think very many conservative pundits have been reminding folks they don't just have to look at the left and feel impotent as they shout and loot their way to everything they want. I felt moved to provide a little push, a little reminder that sometimes you have to decide where you draw the line and then defend that line.

My friend and colleague, Katie Pavlich—Fox News contributor, *Townhall* editor, and professional pretty lady—hit me up immediately after the column published.

"Kira! This needs to be a book!" she virtually shouted over a DM.

She threw me for a loop. A book? Me? I'm a column writer. I write in fits and bursts, about lots of different things. I find it amazing anyone wants to read a thousand words from me, let alone fifty thousand. The thing about Katie is I have never known her to be anything but sincere. She wouldn't have reached out to me like that if she didn't mean what she said; and Katie is someone I respect in the industry. If she thought it would be a good idea, then perhaps it was worth a shot.

I'm so glad she reached out to me that day. As I was writing this book, I began thinking about all the conservatives like me out there, who feel beat up, disenfranchised, and confused about the current confused state of our confused society. I receive messages and emails from people every week, telling me they feel helpless in the face of all the turmoil of the past two years. They want to help, they want to protect, and they even want to change, but they just don't know where to start.

I think the message encompassed in these pages is needed. I think conservatives need encouragement, need reminding they aren't powerless; and I think we all need to be reminded that we've been far too comfortable for far too long, and we are paying the price for that unchecked comfort.

WARNINGS AND DEFINITIONS BEFORE WE GET STARTED

I first want to clarify a couple of things.

You'll see me using the term "progressive" a lot. In some rare cases I will use "liberal." It is important for you to know that in my mind, a liberal and a progressive are not the same thing. I consider a progressive more like an "alt-left" ideologue, a growing and rabid fringe. They rarely pause for reason or compromise. Occasionally I will use the terms interchangeably. The way left-wing people look at the "alt-right" is exactly how I view the "alt-left." When I use the term "liberal" I am simply referring to those who identify politically as left-of-center. Some conservatives might refer to them as "classical liberals." These are the people who definitely don't share my ideology or beliefs but aren't maniacs about it. They believe in heated discussion and the power of persuasion. They love their country, and they make no apologies for their bias, just as conservatives make no such apologies. What I'm trying to say is that they're normal.

Liberal friends, if you're reading this, please know I am not talking about you. I am talking about the progressive fringe lunatics who have managed to push their way into the mainstream of left-wing politics, effectively pushing out more and more reasonable liberals. I try to be clear about the difference. My apologies if sometimes I don't always get it right. Also, as you read, understand this book is not written for you. I have something for you, hopefully in the near future, but this is not it. So, as you feel your blood start to boil at my missives and descriptions and calls to action, try to remind yourself you are not the target audience for this book. This book is for conservatives. I'm speaking their language, addressing their concerns, and drawing on their shared political experiences. Try to keep that in mind as you read. It will make things easier for you.

THE NOISY SEASON

We should be a people of ideological peace. It's what we should want, anyway. These constant battles are draining, and I think most conservatives are feeling exhausted with it all these days. Peace is good, and it's what we all look to when it comes to the future for our children; but sometimes peace cannot simply be willed, it must be wrestled. Bold action feels distasteful for a lot of average conservatives, but we need only to look at our left-wing counterparts to see how effective it can be. We're going to have to accept that a peaceful coexistence with our ideological opponents will have to be won, it will not be given.

The trickle is starting but we need to create a roaring river, a current of good sense. It is time to put diplomacy on pause. It has its place, and for those of us still engaged in public debate and discussion, we should never completely abandon it. Persuasion is a vital part of winning any culture war. There is value in walking softly, but sometimes persuasion can only be made palatable to the other side by carrying a big stick.

So, draw your line. Decide where it is. It won't be the same for all of us. Your line will be different from my line and that's okay. The battle has many fronts. But it's important to understand this: The quiet season is over. We are in a noisy season. Grab a bullhorn and start screaming.

CHAPTER 1

WOMEN'S RIGHTS AND THE TRANSGENDER MOVEMENT

Few social contagions have enjoyed more rapid expansion than the transgender movement. Ten years ago it would have been unthinkable to put a boy in a sports bra and force his way onto a girls soccer team. Now girls are being suspended from their own teams for daring to protest boys walking on to their teams and dominating their sports. Title IX—built to protect women against discrimination in academia, athletics, and other professional and educational arenas that receive federal funding—is collapsing under the weight of a misogynist movement that dons a dress and lipstick and calls itself "equality."

HOW DID WE GET HERE?

The slippery slope

The progressive left in this country does not believe there is a such thing as a slippery slope. They think that is solely a construct of the political right, a fantasy old White men dreamt up in the smoking lounges of exclusive, men-only country clubs, as they sip expensive scotch, torsos draped in velvet robes, grouching nonstop about how things "used to be." They can think this because the hallmark of the progressive left's mind-set is the ability to memory-hole history. They can spend enormous amounts of energy ridiculing and raging against Donald Trump for claiming his reelection was manipulated and stolen, while somehow having no memory at all of Hillary Clinton and her supporters claiming for four years that the election of 2016 was manipulated and stolen.

They can hail the late Senator John McCain as a "maver-ick" hero for preventing the final nail in the coffin of Obam-acare. They can praise him for being the anti-Republican Republican and write glowing think pieces on his bravery and leadership, while somehow having no memory at all about the horrible way they treated him when he was running against Barrack Obama for the highest office in the land. McCain was accused of being a feeble, racist, dangerous Nazi sympathizer who did everything but kill puppies. No, that was an accusation they saved for their other new favorite Republican son, Mitt Romney. The progressive left has successfully forgotten their absolute disdain for the Romneys and their claims that not only were they as awful and racist as their Republican predecessors, they were basically puppy-killers. Romney (for some weird reason) told a funny "I'm just like you" story about how they used to put their pup in a crate tied to the top of their car when they would go on family road trips. After that he was not only a Jim Crow sympathizing, racist Republican . . . he was a serial dog abuser, which is just about the worst thing you can be these days, right behind someone who refuses to pretend biology doesn't exist.

Have you seen their take on George Bush lately? I'm old enough to remember when George Bush was the worst person in the world, according to the left wing. He was a warmonger, a greedy oil baron, and the reason we were attacked on 9/11. His twin daughters were mercilessly picked apart in the media for the crime of being teenagers. He was the devil incarnate who "stole" an election with hanging chads and a cabal of Deep State minions. He was the first president I recall getting the "literally Hitler" treatment. The way some people described President Bush for eight years was heinous and calculatedly cold. There was no room for nuance. It was nonstop, wall-to-wall, daily, hourly criticism from the left—not just the alt-left that is represented by the increasingly crazed progressive crowd, but liberals in general. He was blamed for not transforming into a dictator and taking over the city of New Orleans to render aid during Hurricane Katrina. The things said about his intentions and actions regarding that storm and the breaking of the levees that ended up sinking parts of New Orleans were truly the most harsh, vile things I have ever heard uttered about a sitting president.

In a sneak preview into the chaotic mind of one of the most hailed artists in the world, Kanye West cohosted a segment of a charity telethon with actor Mike Meyers and infamously (and bizarrely) blurted out, apropos of nothing, *"George Bush hates Black people!"* If you are one of those problematic people who memory-holes your own inconvenient narratives, then perhaps you don't remember this, in which case I implore you to look up the clip, not for Kanye, but for the reaction of his cohost Mike Meyers. It was a live national broadcast, at a time when streaming platforms had not yet become a part of daily life. It seemed as though everyone in the country was watching this telethon. Meyers, who is not a political celebrity and certainly wasn't prepared for the outburst, was frozen in horror. It remains perhaps one of the funniest things I've ever seen on live television.

All that to say that George Bush was accused of being a dictator and evil patriarch and it was merciless and endless coming from the left. Now he's just a quaint, cute old man who paints pictures and hangs out with the Obamas.

So yes, it is incredibly easy to deny a slippery slope exists when you don't even have a memory of the hill behind you, and you never look back to see where you've come from.

Those on the right perhaps could be accused of employing the worry of slippery slopes a bit too liberally (pun intended). There's certainly no denying that we talk about it a lot. I recall going to see Dinesh D'Souza's documentary on Barrack Obama in 2012. It was about where the deliberately destructive plans of the Obama administration would lead us, culminating in what could be a terrifying and apocalyptic collapse in 2016. Obama was painted as nothing less than a dictator who may actually be willing to suspend elections and declare himself an emperor.

While I can already hear some people reading this passage and running down a list their minds of all the ways he damaged this country irreparably, if we can be reasonable for a moment, we can at least all agree that America did not crumble, the apocalypse did not descend, and Obama left office peacefully (albeit, with a lot of salt in his mouth). Perhaps D'Souza was overstating things just a bit for the big screen. America did indeed survive the Obama years.

I'm a big believer in self-awareness as a tool of logic. We on the right bear a good share of the blame for overreacting when we should be reasoning, and thus adding to the sense of hostility in discourse.

Regardless, we're not making up the slippery slope. It exists and we're sliding down it in real time.

The vertical drop

When the battle over gay marriage was still raging in this country, many conservatives stood in opposition on religious and moral grounds, but others opposed the notion for fear it might send us into a spiral of never-ending identity groups asking for the same accommodations. The argument was that while it certainly shouldn't matter to any other individual who you decide to call your husband or wife, changing the legal definition of an historical constant could lead to a chaotic decline in order. They were, of course, scoffed at and shamed as hysterical bigots. Some may well have been, but many were making at the very least a salient argument that deserved to be aired out and looked at. Legalizing same-sex unions under federal law was one thing, changing the very definition of the word "marriage" was quite another.

Fast-forward to 2021, a mere 20–25 years after the Lesbian and Gay lobby told us, "We're normal people, just like you and we want normalized recognition of our romantic impulses, just like you. We're average Americans who just want to be left to live our lives as normally as possible." They've since added bisexuality and transsexuality to their monikers and suddenly the LGBTQ lobby is in the business of redefining the scientific, biological constants of gender.

The slippery slope turned into a straight vertical drop within two decades.

In the beginning of the madness, I was happy to continue with my philosophy of grace, and live and let live. If you feel as though your physical appearance is not in line with your emotional state, who am I to judge? You do you. The truth is, I was just as terrified of being labeled as a homophobe and bigot as the next person. Some of my closest friends are gay, and while they're certainly not transgender, they reside in the same political and social strata and are aligned. To question the logic of transgender ideology is to question the gay rights movement in general, and that is heresy. I never wanted to come off as intolerant or thoughtless to the people I loved and if they were in league with this new transgender philosophy, well surely the very least I could do is throw up my hands and say, "None of my business, no judgment."

As it turned out, however, there are a couple of problems with that approach, and I admit that my capitulation to the philosophy (the tenacity of which I grossly underestimated) was naïve. I believed my attitude of live and let live would act as an anchor of sorts. I let my fear of rejection cloud my judgment.

I have a teenage daughter and we live in Southern California. We are Hollywood-adjacent. She goes to school with the children of celebrities. Many of her classmates and peers over the years have been YouTube stars and TikTok personalities. She is surrounded by a constant barrage of materialism and narcissism.

As a result, we often find ourselves discussing the scourge of eating disorders in her school, and how to avoid being sucked into that mindset. I don't praise anorexia to my daughter. I don't tell her, "Oh don't worry about those friends of yours who are bulimic. Live and let live. As long as they're not bothering anyone, what's the big deal?" To do so would be ridiculous. It would be encouraging chaotic thinking for her.

If the image in the mirror is completely different from the image in your mind, something is wrong with you. If you see your 99-pound frame as "fat," something is wrong with you. It is dysmorphia. It is a lie your mind tells you about your body. No one thinks anorexics should be normalized or left alone to their own devices and no one thinks they are just fat people born in the wrong bodies. We all recognize it as a mental health and severe physical issue requiring treatment and patience. Every reasonable person agrees.

The transsexual movement successfully attached itself (without merit, I believe, but that's another story for the LGB community to tell) to the gay rights movement and managed to fold their gender issues into lesbian and gay activism. They rebranded from transsexual to transgender. Taking the notion of sexual deviancy out of the trans brand allowed them to piggyback onto the gay rights movement, which at the time of the trans takeover, was on the cusp of securing the thing those early activists had said they wanted—normalcy.

The trans brand cannot coexist peacefully with the LGB brand. Gay "philosophy" or gay-affirming values still depend on the biological separation of genders. In fact, biology is the cornerstone of gay acceptance. If gender and sexuality are fluid, then there can be no such thing as gay, only varying degrees of gender and varying degrees of sexual attraction. The entire case for gay normalcy has always rested on the branding of gay as something you are born to be. If gender is simply a social construct, then no one can be born with a genetic coding to be attracted to one gender or another. The gay lobby has always insisted that homosexuality falls on the "nature" end of the nature vs. nurture scale. The transgender activists they've welcomed into the movement erase that notion entirely. Those troublesome Christian conservatives have always been considered the problem when it comes to gay Americans accepting their own sexuality and being accepted for it. They refused to see the "nature" end of the issue and instead painted homosexuality as a perversion of our default heterosexuality.

The "T" in LGBT has completely laid waste to that argument. It is a surprising irony few people saw coming. The gay rights advocates—so sure their biggest enemy was the Christian conservative—have ended up embracing the one philosophy that could erase their decades of work altogether. They have embraced their own demise. The T came in as an ally but looks more and more like a Trojan horse.

The transgender movement has been clever to tie their fate to the gay rights movement—a movement that has been hugely successful and frankly remains an effective model for growing an activist movement. One of the greatest tools of any effective movement is shame. Gay activists were able to attach shame to the notion of disapproval of homosexual activity and lifestyle. No one likes to be thought of as mean or intolerant. Whether or not you approve of this tactic, it is patently obvious it has been extremely effective.

By attaching itself to that very effective strategy, the trans movement was able to take advantage of the current climate surrounding sexuality and shaming people who don't wish to be coerced into accepting the latest and greatest when it comes to gender/sexual ideology. Now we find ourselves in the very bizarre place of facing shame and criticism simply for asserting the biological reality of the male and female forms. And who is on the losing end of this madness?

Women, of course

Sixty years after my mother's generation burned their bras in defiance of social norms while demanding equal treatment for women, we now find ourselves in a situation she and her peers would have found unthinkable after the tumult of the '60s.

Democrat leaders love to tell us every single election cycle that if this Republican or that one is elected it will set back civil rights 100 years . . . or 150 years. Or 200 years. Pick a number.

It changes every cycle, not that it matters to the incurious voter. If anyone actually took the time to sit and think about just how a Republican president would reinstitute slavery and how that would even pass muster in a society that is armed to the teeth and has already gone to war once over the issue, they would realize the idea is ridiculous on its face. But logic is not a strong suit of the far-left progressive set. If it were, they would see that the greatest modern threat to civil rights is already on our doorstep and in fact is already reversing decades of progress.

I am speaking, of course, about the civil rights of women. And again, I can't help but hearken back to the bra-burning hippies who demanded that women be given fair and equal treatment outside of the home. They surely didn't imagine their efforts would one day be in vain. They certainly didn't imagine it would be their own liberal allies who would eventually betray the women's rights movement.

While Democrats and progressives scream hysterically about the imaginary erosion of civil rights for Black voters, a very real erosion of civil rights is happening right under their noses. The boldness with which has been particularly shocking.

This madness has already gone way too far. "Gender dysphoria" is becoming a bigoted term. Young men and women experiencing dysphoria are being directed to make life-altering, body-altering choices without regard to psychological treatment and therapy. There is nothing healthy or sane about cutting off healthy, normal reproductive organs as a way to satiate the need for one's mental image of oneself to match the physical image.

The transgender community has made being a woman something to be ashamed of, on both sides of that fence. Trans "men" see the female shape as abhorrent. We look at the ancient Chinese practice of foot binding for women as cruel and sexist, a tale of warning against succumbing to the patriarchy's idea of femininity. We laugh at their obsession. And yet here we are in twenty-first-century America, passing out chest binders to young women who think they are men, so they can squash their perfectly healthy breasts out of existence. We put them on unnecessary hormones that will have irreversible consequences for the rest of their lives. We let teachers and medical professionals—people they are supposed to trust for help—tell them the only way to feel good about who they are is to mutilate their form, that the ideal form for them is a male form, that if they find their female form repulsive it can only be because they were simply never female to begin with. They are allowed to treat womanhood with disdain, and then they wonder aloud why women are still often treated so disrespectfully in the public square. They've made a cottage industry out of that complaint, even as they encourage women to abandon womanhood altogether.

We're supposed to be slaves to the binary when a girl has her vagina voluntarily sewn shut but when conservatives want to talk about the very real differences between men and women, we're all supposed to get on board the "gender is a social construct" train.

And on the other side of the equation, we have trans "women," men who insist they were born into the wrong body. They have been even more aggressive than women who "transition" to the male binary. They have also been the most insulting to women. They live their entire lives with their male privilege, navigating the world as men and being benefited by the world as men. Then one day they change their name and declare themselves a woman and we women are expected to immediately treat them as such.

Conversely, there don't seem to be many women out there yelling at men that they must accept them as men now that they have stubble and cargo pants. Frankly, men don't generally seem to care all that much. Why should they? There is nothing about a woman becoming a man that is threatening to any man. Her presence requires no changing of any definitions for them. She can't dominate a man in any way. She can't push a man off the men's soccer team. She can't take his place in any real physical aspects. In fact, from what we've seen, trans "men" are not on the loud end of the movement. At most they may grace an article in *The Daily Mail UK*, asking us to pretend a man actually gave birth. *"Man gives birth as lover undergoes transition surgery in the next room!"* You know the headlines. Or am I the only one who gets trapped in the *Daily Mail* sidebar rabbit hole for hours on end?

You'll notice when Ben Shapiro or Jordan Peterson appears on a program to debate transgender ideology, they are nearly exclusively arguing with male-to-female transitioners. The battle surrounding transgenderism is nearly always framed in terms of women making room for trans "women" and allowing children to choose their gender. The men don't seem to have any issues at all with female-to-male transitioners.

Trans women have been the aggressors of the movement. And that's because they are men; and many weak-willed men who don't get what they want become aggressive. Oftentimes that aggression is aimed at the "weaker sex." So, while the men on the other side of this battle continue their lives relatively unaffected by women who barge into their gender, women find themselves on the losing end of an aggressive campaign aimed at silencing their concerns.

My mother definitely did not burn her bra for this.

The *Mad Men* stereotype of misogyny is a bunch of men sitting around in suits and ties, sipping bourbon and objectifying women. They laugh when a woman tries to express an idea, they tell her she doesn't know what she's talking about, and they kick her out of the room. Her very presence is unnecessary if it's not affirming their masculinity in some way. She's serving you or she's screwing you. End of story.

Misogyny is alive and thriving in the transgender movement, and it should come as no surprise that men haven't changed much over the years. Now instead of sitting around conference tables, they sit around social media. Instead of sipping bourbon, they take hormone treatments. Instead of suits and ties, they wear dresses. They're still telling us we don't know what we're talking about and still ridiculing us when we try to voice our concerns. They still send us out of the room if we're not affirming their gender ideology. We're still simply objects to them, only in this iteration we are objectified for our gender rather than for a man's sexual appetite. Teenage girls are bullied for speaking up about their fears and insecurities surrounding allowing boys into their female spaces at schools. They are being harassed for asking boys calling themselves girls not be allowed to dominate their sports, or push them out of the running for awards and scholarships.

Even great heroines have fallen to the aggressive cancel culture campaign led by men who believe their voices are more valid than a woman's voice.

J. K. Rowling is a hero to many people of all political stripes. She went from a single mom on the dole to one of the best-selling authors of all time. Her stories are responsible for the employment of thousands of people over the years, and for the celebrity and riches of several actors. She's a liberal and a gay rights activist. We know she was on the "right" side of things because she hated Donald Trump. What other liberal bona fides do you need?

But even Rowling herself, with all her money and all her influence, was not above the criticism of the aggressive transgender crowd when she took umbrage to a magazine article that identified women as "people who menstruate."[1]

> If sex isn't real, there's no same-sex attraction. If sex isn't real, the lived reality of women globally is erased. I know and love trans people, but erasing the concept of sex removes the ability of many to meaningfully discuss their lives. It isn't hate to speak the truth. The idea that women like me, who've been empathetic to trans people for decades, feeling kinship because they're vulnerable in the same way as women—i.e., to male violence—"hate" trans people because they think sex is real and has lived consequences—is a nonsense. I respect every trans person's right to live any way that feels authentic and comfortable to them. I'd march with you if you were discriminated against on the basis of being trans. At

the same time, my life has been shaped by being
female. I do not believe it's hateful to say so.[2]

She was raked over the coals by the online mob, including
many of the very people she made rich and famous. They took
the side of the men over her. They told her she should shut up.
They told her she should rethink her womanhood. All she said
was that she didn't want womanhood to be erased on the
altar of gender theory. She stood up for women and was
shouted down.

Does any of this sound familiar?

The thing is, Rowling can stand up to the heat. She's rich,
she'll never need another job again, she's well established in
her peer group. She has no more ladders to climb in her field
and thus no one to stop her. She doesn't need to worry about
the next promotion or the next opportunity. I'm not suggesting
she never worries. She's a human with goals and dreams like
everyone else; but her livelihood isn't on the line. She can
afford to be "canceled."

What about the rest of us?

If you have the luxury of being "cancel proof" and you believe
in the right of women to define themselves and have their
voices heard in the public square, you have the duty to stand
up and say something now, before it's too late. We women
need you. These aggressors get to control the conversation
because they've attached themselves to the power of the gay
rights movement. Their power is inherited but it is not mer-
ited. In reality, there are more people who believe this is an
affront not only to our created beings, but to the rights of
women everywhere. There are more of us, but we need to exert
some power here. That means we need many more Rowlings.

It's important to note that Rowling is by no means a conservative. She is a proud liberal who regularly advocates for gay
rights and agendas. This should be an encouraging sign for us.
We have allies in this arena, and if we can learn to set aside

other political issues when addressing this problem, we can marshal a lot of resources and a lot of power. However, people like me don't always know the big players in high places. I'm just a stay-at-home mother who decided to get involved in political punditry and activism. I grew up in humble circumstances. I've scraped for every dollar and scrapped for every opportunity. I have a pulpit, but I'm not necessarily connected. If you are one of the fortunate few to be "cancel proof," people like me desperately need people like you. If you can't speak, think about funding the efforts of those who can.

That being said, if you have even the slightest inclination to speak up, please do. It is literally now or never. The time is fast approaching when we will be punished by the force of government for not capitulating to this insanity. It has already infiltrated some areas of government and academia.

You will not be taking on a political issue; you will be defending the very future of your own descendants. For what will happen to free and prosperous society if we succumb to this madness? Peace cannot coexist with chaos. Right now, the chaos is closing in all around us. Will you stand up and push it back? Will you defend the borders of peace?

WHERE ARE THE MEN?

Where are you? There are a couple of big names in the political sphere who have stood up for women. Ben Shapiro comes to mind immediately. YouTube celebrity Steven Crowder has been quite vocal about the reality of biology and the transgender movement. There are a few other big names who have achieved enough success so as to be "uncancelable," but most of them argue in the arena of academic application of gender theory, or the arena of biology (all legitimate arenas). Where are the men standing up to *protect* women?

Conservative men are very clear about the complimentary roles of women. They are often extremely proud to be fathers and husbands, supports to their wives and mothers and daughters. They see themselves as protectors, charged with keeping nefarious forces at bay in order to give their families the best chance for success.

Yet, when it comes to pushing back against the transgender takeover of womanhood, so many conservative men seem to be silent. Oh sure, they complain about it on social media and in like-minded company. They are rarely seen in public pushing back. Too many of you out there are leaving it to the women to push out the men trying to silence them. It's almost as if you've internally accepted these men are actually women and you don't want to be seen as bullying women. Meanwhile, the women are being bullied regularly, shouted down and told we don't count as women if we're not toeing the transgender line. Abigail Shrier, J. K. Rowling, Bridget Phetasy, the mom down the street . . . women everywhere are on the frontlines of pushing back against their own erasure, but sometimes it feels like we've been abandoned by the very men who claim they are protectors and respecters of femininity. We need you to get loud.

I can already hear the arguments. I've heard them many times over.

"Kira, we would but men aren't even allowed to have opinions in public anymore when it comes to anything to do with women. We are shouted down, shamed, and called misogynists. Sometimes we are threatened with #MeToo–type allegations that are nothing but vindictive. Our opinions are not welcome."

First, welcome to the club! Second, the time to speak up and speak out isn't when it's easy and all the conditions are right. The time to speak up is when you see trouble on the horizon. The time to speak up is when things begin to get scary. The time to speak up is now. Many of you would kill to protect us, many of you would give your lives to protect us. How many of you would give your career or your reputation or your personal interests to protect us? What are you willing to risk fighting for the women in your life? Why are you leaving it to us to do alone? We're fighting a battle with the physical and societal odds stacked against us. You're asking us to stand up to men in an arena meant for women. They are often twice our physiological size, twice as bold (all those years of male privilege stack up), and twice as aggressive (again, a necessary male quality that sometimes gets perverted when narcissistic men don't get their way). You would never leave us to do that in any other circumstance. How can you abandon us now?

We need more men to take more risks on our behalf. I'm sorry you've been shouted down and marginalized for "male privilege," but how much of that happens because it's out of your control and how much of that happens because you've been content to live and let live?

There's no more room for live and let live. Not right now. Perhaps one day we can return to that, but it is clear now the other side of this equation has no intention of letting us live as we please, while demanding we let them live as they please and actively approve of their choices. It's time for men to get uncomfortable. It's one thing for the Jordan Petersons of the world to argue against trans ideology as a matter of biology or in an academic sense. He takes more than his fair share of slings and arrows for it, to be sure. But sometimes we don't need a professor to argue the merits of gender. We need a man to stand up and say, "You are bullying these women and I won't hear of it. Back off!"

Too many of you are leaving us to be the ones to stand up in a man's face and tell him he can't be a woman if he doesn't have a vagina. Don't think we don't get intimidated by the specter of a man taking on a female form and demanding we accept his definition of our gender.

The progressive left has been bellyaching for decades about the embedded misogyny of the patriarchy and how men are constantly trying to tell women what to do with their bodies, their careers, etc. Well, here is a group of men telling women what a woman is, silencing the fears and traumas of women, and even scooping up awards and coveted athletic spots in place of women.

Misogyny, thy name is transgender.

Think about how it felt to see Bruce-now-Caitlyn Jenner put on a dress, tuck in his penis and then, after being a "woman" for all of a month, go out and accept an ESPN award for Woman of the Year? Jenner hadn't even been a woman *for* a year. You may recall that event. Jenner came on stage to a standing ovation. The only person who refused to acknowledge the theatrics was Brett Favre and for that he was excoriated in the liberal press. He wouldn't clap and became public enemy #1 for a time. He was the only man there with the testicles to refuse to diminish womanhood by pretending this person in front of him had earned anything at all as a woman.

Bitch, bossy, Karen, Felicia, whore . . . there are a myriad of insulting labels for women who annoy us, but there are hardly any male equivalents. We often find ourselves denigrated and insulted for getting loud or getting angry. Men don't typically have this problem. It's easy for progressives, in all their misogyny, to label angry women as "problematic" shrews. It is purposefully dismissive. We need our men standing next to us and frankly, in front of us. I've seen far too little of that, but the time has come to make a choice.

You can be scared of the mob or stand up to the mob. What would you risk for your daughter or your wife?

Women and girls are already being sacrificed on the altar of this illusion. In California, imprisoned men are taking advantage of new transgender laws that allow them to be moved to a women's facility if they identify as a woman. This might be somewhere on the far edges of acceptable if these men were first required to undergo treatment and evaluation, but they are not. They are simply allowed to request a transfer based on their chosen identity. Only a fool would believe no man would take advantage of this loophole. Indeed, we are already seeing reports of female inmates experiencing sexual assaults from male prisoners who identify as women.[3] The #MeToo movement graced us with "Believe all women," and yet these women are routinely ignored and their reports are suppressed by government and media.

Once again, the needs and desires of men are valued above the safety of women. We cannot take any of these people seriously when they tell us they are concerned about equality for women. They are the ones silencing women as they suffer the terrible consequences of gender ideology—or more to the point, gender theology—in real time. Many of these women are in prison because of events surrounding serious trauma in their lives. Some of those traumas led them to a life of crime, some of those traumas caused them to lash out. Now they are being victimized all over again, with nary a peep from the social justice warriors in the media. Where are the men who will stand for these women? Where are the men who will protect these women?

If you don't stand up now, what you'll end up with is Loudoun County right at your doorstep. In a case that received national attention only after a year of being covered up by the school board, a young girl was raped in a high school bathroom. Her assaulter was a boy who had previously been suspended for sexual assault. The boy accessed the girl's bathroom by claiming to be transgender. This isn't to say he would not have found a way to assault girls even without their ridiculous bathroom policy in place, but it certainly did give him a "safe haven" to abuse his classmates.

To add insult to injury, the people elected to serve and protect this young woman covered up the crime.[4] They prioritized their social agenda over the health and safety of their students. It wasn't until the irate father of the victim showed up at a meeting to excoriate the school board that anyone took notice. That poor girl languished in neglect and shame for over a year before any adult in charge even admitted it happened. The girl's father was hauled off like a criminal.

It never should have gotten to that point. Men, your daughters are at risk. Don't wait for the worst to happen. Don't subject yourselves and your daughters to this unimaginable pain and outrage. We can't wait until it is too late. Our children cannot afford it.

There are some people reading this who are right this very second fixing their mouths to say, "Kira, only a small minority of trans people are like this. Most of us just want to be left alone to live our lives quietly and we don't want to force you into accepting our choices. We really do want to live and let live."

Of course, there are transgender people out there who speak out against the fascism of this current iteration of the sexual revolution. Blair White is an extremely popular YouTuber and transgender female who advocates for the victims of sexual abuse and regularly calls out pedophilia in trans, gay, and online communities. She (I will use the preferred pronoun on this occasion) is an amazing voice for sanity, and while I have no doubt White would prefer it if I weren't always putting quotations around "woman," she doesn't really care what I do because her self-worth is not tied up in what I approve of in regards to herself. On top of that, White values free thought and free expression above gender theory.

So, do I know there are trans people are out there who stand with sanity? Yes, but what are the rest of you doing?

I don't want to hear about how you hate this stuff too. If you identify as a man, then act like one. Start protecting us from the erasure of womanhood. If you identify as a woman, then you should be as bothered by this as the rest of us. Were you truly a woman you would be vocal. You would be angry, because that's how women get when they are dismissed and abused. Don't sit there and just shrug and tell me "Oh, I feel the same way you do." No, you don't. If you did, you'd be yelling just as loudly. Start making some noise or stop lying to us and yourselves.

We have a moral duty to our daughters, and we need men to stand with us. We need "heroic masculinity." The women are already doing the heavy lifting here. It is time for men to step up in large numbers and start pulling this weight.

WHAT IS A WOMAN?

What does it truly mean to be a woman? There are a lot of emotional and psychological features common to women, but we would all agree those are often malleable and debatable.

Women are cautious investors, women are nurturers, women tend to value emotional connection over physical connection. Any therapist worth their salt can verify this. Even a financial advisor knows these qualities. But if I sit down and really think about "what is a woman?" I find myself at a loss for direct descriptions. There are all kinds of ideas and qualities to explore, but in the end, the definition of a woman has to be biological, and then everything else fans out from there.

A woman has breasts. A woman has a vagina. A woman has a menstrual cycle. A woman creates ovum. A woman has the ability to gestate and birth children. These are all incredibly specific female qualities. The transgender activists try to use the argument that there are plenty of women who don't possess these qualities and are women anyway. Some women have their wombs removed, some are infertile, some don't get a period, some have their breast removed for health reasons like cancer treatment. If we still consider them women, we must extend that definition to men who identify as women. After all, their bodies simply have those same limitations.

That is a lie. A woman is not simply a body absent of male genitalia. A woman is supposed to be fertile, supposed to have breasts, supposed to have a womb. If for some reason these qualities are absent in her body, she sees a physician . . . because it isn't natural.

I can remember when my daughter was approaching the age when her menstrual cycle would kick in. Like many girls, she was feeling anxiety about it (this is another experience unique to women and not men or trans "women"). One day I told her, "I know it seems scary, but this is a normal bodily development for women. In fact, it is so normal that if for some reason you don't develop a cycle, I will have to take you to the doctor to find out what is wrong with your body."

An infertile woman still must deal with the reality of her infertility as a woman. A woman forced to have her breasts removed will struggle with the reality of this very womanly feature being taken from her, and what it means for her sexuality and for her health. The removal of a woman's womb is no small thing. It has other lasting consequences for how her body will function, and the psychological burden is very real. In short, it is not an acceptable argument to suppose a man can be a woman simply because some women don't have the physical function of the female form. To not have these things is not natural for a woman's body and to be absent of these qualities simply adds another layer to the complexity of womanhood. It alleviates nothing.

A woman's body is so uniquely complex that there is an entire medical profession dedicated to our intricate biology.

So no, simply saying you're a woman because you feel like you are is not an acceptable standard. How do you know you feel like a woman? How do women feel? What do women feel? When I wake up in the morning I do not say "I feel like a woman today" (Cue Shania Twain). I simply . . . am.

The current iteration of the LGBT-add-whatever-letters-you-like movement cannot sustain this logic. They push for gender neutral toy and clothing sections at department stores (now the law here in California) because they say it is inexcusable to stereotype the desires and personalities of children. Never mind the marketing is based on extensive research into what girls and boys like. They think it is dangerous to stereotype girls and boys. Girls can play with trucks. Boys can play with Barbies.

Yet when the "T" enters the picture, we're suddenly asked to believe a man decided he was a woman because he likes dresses and makeup. Are we stereotyping or is gender fluid? The logic folds in on itself upon examination. It is up to us to force these people to examine their assumptions. After all, isn't that what they are demanding we do?

That can be a two-way street, and frankly if we don't make it one, we will soon find ourselves in the nightmare Democrats have been promising us at the feet of Republicans for decades: rolling back civil rights 100 years.

This is nothing more than the complete erasure of womanhood at the behest of men who don't like that they cannot control or dictate womanhood. Why does "equality" for women always seem to mean just erasing everything that makes being a woman special?

In my heart, I believe this isn't just a battle against "societal norm." This is a concerted effort to devalue life. That's why women are the most common victims of transgender theology. We are the carriers of life. Whether we have the privilege to bear life or not, the very notion of what it means to bring forth life is wrapped within our DNA.

It is a holy endowment. This is not just a battle for our bathrooms. This is a battle to preserve the order of God's creation, and the special place He has given women in the propagation of the human race. It's a battle for life.

We should defend ourselves from this onslaught of illogic and erasure with the same passion we defend babies from the horrors of abortion. They are intimately connected concepts that circle around the same divine center: life.

WHAT CAN YOU DO?

Show up

This whole book is about showing up. Showing up to council meetings, school board meetings, company diversity meetings—anywhere you think you're not wanted when it comes to this discussion, show up. Make yourself seen and heard. Be kind, be gracious, be impassioned, be outraged, be whatever you want. Just show up. The reason the progressives have been able to get away with this for so long is because we've simply abandoned these spaces to them. We find their worldview extremely distasteful, and we'd rather not bathe in it. Unfortunately, that has left them alone to be as crazy as they want to be. The adults left the room for a few decades and when we returned, we discovered the kids had resorted to cannibalism.

During the Summer O' BLM when statues and traditions were being torn down and burned to the ground, I received a lot of concerned emails from conservatives. They were scared about these big changes in the landscape of American patriotism. They were outraged our history was being erased in front of our eyes. They were disgusted those ideologues were being allowed to essentially tear down American history and rebuild it in their own image.

I shared a lot of their concerns, but one piece of advice I gave consistently was this: change is here. Our country is always changing and that's a good thing. If you're scared of the change, don't let the change happen to you—be a part of the change. Figure out a way to be a part of the discussions, the panels, the protests, the townhalls. Be a voice for reason. Instead of abandoning the battleground in frustration, engage. These people think they have the exclusive right to say and do whatever they want. That's because we've given it to them as we've retreated to our own safe spaces—red states, family, cloistered social media. That's why the left gets so upset when we start making noise. They literally think they own the right to shout and protest, and that is our fault. So, get into those spaces where you think you don't belong and let everyone know you are now a part of the discussion, and they'll damn well have to deal with it. We can make the coming change lean our way, or theirs. Change is coming either way—so which way would you prefer it to lean?

Refuse to comply

I know this is a hard one. This is truly advice requiring the rubber to meet the road. I have no judgment for anyone who chooses to comply while silently cursing the lunacy. Your job is at stake, sometimes your most treasured relationships, your reputation. If you have a family to support, that changes how you view when and where you'll stand up. If you can, refuse. There is strength in numbers, so consider finding other like-minded people and forming a support network.

It can be scary, but you'd be surprised at how often the opposition will acquiesce to those who hold their ground. In the end, the Constitution really is on your side, even if it gets muted by the social justice fascists.

Take the case of Tanner Cross. Cross was a Loudoun County, Virginia, physical education teacher who announced his non-compliance at a school board meeting in 2021. In a short but thoughtful speech, he told the board he had no intention of violating his faith or lying to his students to support a political agenda.

> My name is Tanner Cross, and I am speaking out of love for those who suffer with gender dysphoria. "60 Minutes" this past Sunday interviewed over 30 young people who transitioned, but they felt led astray because lack of pushback, or how easy it was to make physical changes to their bodies in just three months. They are now detransitioning. It's not my intention to hurt anyone, but there are certain truths we must face when ready. We condemn policies like 8040 and 8035 because it was damaged children, defile the holy image of God. I love all of my students but I would never lie to them regardless of the consequences. I'm a teacher, but I serve God first. And I will not affirm a biological boy can be a girl and vice-versa because it's against my religion it's lying to a child. It's abuse to a child and it's sinning against our God.[5]

Cross was suspended immediately, but he did not apologize, and he did not beg for his job. Instead, he secured a lawyer and dared the school board to fire him. They played a months' long game of chicken, but eventually the school board caved. At the time of this book's publication, Tanner Cross is still gainfully employed as a teacher in Loudoun County public schools.

He made the choice to risk his livelihood. This time it panned out, but in other situations it doesn't. I know that. The decision as to what and how much you'll risk is yours, but the truth is the progressive left in government can only do to us what we allow them to do.

Write your reps

I know, this sounds like a mantra. That's fine. It is.

One of the most surprising discoveries I've made in my time as a pundit and activist is that your letters and calls really do make a lot of difference to your elected officials. It happens so rarely these days that often when they do get just a few hundred communications on a single issue, it can sway their voting. Most elected officials have only one goal: to be reelected. The fact you take the time to call or write tells them you'll take the time to go to the ballot box too—and they want to be sure you go to that ballot box for them. It doesn't work every time, but it works more than you think. Keep reminding these people you are watching them, and you have expectations.

Own the businesses, run the panels, be the diversity officers, be the system

This isn't too different from the first point I made in this section. Put yourself on the committee assigned to hire a "diversity consultant" and then look for consultants who might be more inclined to your political bent. They are out there, believe it or not.

Start being strategic. You are not helpless. I don't know why we've allowed ourselves to assume we don't have a say in these things. We do. Yes, you will be judged and shouted at and talked about. As I've been discussing, there is a certain amount of risk we will have to incur, but isn't life's risks a thing we've been discussing ad nauseum throughout the pandemic and the creeping fascism its encouraged?

Make people tell you that you're not welcome, and then go to human resources and cause trouble, just like they would. This is your workplace, your home, your country. Stand up for it all. Sitting is easier, but if you do it too much you'll never be able to tell when they close the lock on the chains they slipped around your ankles.

CHAPTER 2

SCHOOL CHOICE

*I*was raised by a passionate, rebellious, hippie mother in socialist Canada. When I joined my father in America (he is an American citizen) as a teenager, I became a default Democrat, like many Black Americans. I had many strong and rigid opinions, as most young people do when they have not yet discovered all the ways life can crush your ideals. I was convinced of the typical assertions all Republicans are racists, all conservatives are racists, and the Black community would be restored emotionally and economically if only we could get rid of all those racists on the right. It wasn't until I began to serve my own community that my politics were challenged.

After marriage, I joined my husband in Gary, Indiana. Gary is a majority Black city with a tragically failing economy and high crime statistics. It's nothing like the famous Broadway song that popped into your mind the moment you read the words "Gary, Indiana." My time in Gary represented a sea-change in my life. Though I had lived in inner cities before, Gary brought on a complete paradigm shift.

It's funny the paths God will lead you down if you don't get in the way of your own self too often. I chose faith as a young teenager, and having little familial guidance in that arena, I was happily forced to lean on God for advice and direction. I decided pretty early on in my life to let Him lead me. I'm not great at it. Like most humans, my pride and stubbornness often obscure my awareness of His direction. As I said, I wasn't around a lot of people who shared with me how to discern God's voice. I could only decide to be a follower and be willing to turn in directions that may not make sense to me. To the outsider it might seem strange a country girl from a small rural island would end up spending most of her young adult years in the inner city, but that's exactly what happened in my life.

I officially left Canada for the United States upon graduating high school, and I never really looked back. My time as an American has been the complete opposite of my Canadian life. I found myself taking up residence—completely by accident, to my mind—in inner city areas like North St. Louis. I found some brief breaks of diversity in my time in cities like Nashville and Chicago, but after I married, I relocated to my husband's hometown of Gary, Indiana, and there my life, and my politics changed forever.

This is where I would become a conservative.

Gary wasn't my first introduction into inner city life, but it marked the first time I ever looked at it as my home. Before, I always had a life beyond. I traveled for work, I stayed with friends outside my hood, I explored the country with friends and sometimes on my own. This time I had a home and a family, a church and neighbors I knew and socialized with. I lived there. It was my community. I was embedded. I didn't love it, but home is where the heart is, and since my heart has always been with my husband, home was Gary.

My father-in-law, Victor, had a huge impact on my life. He was the first Black man I'd ever met who openly called himself a conservative and a Republican. He was a pastor and had been serving his city for decades by the time I came into the family. We hit it off right away, but obviously our politics were different. He never pushed me too hard, but always engaged me in discussions and encouraged me to ask questions about a lot of the baseline assumptions I had regarding politics.

It's a longer story for another day but suffice to say, Victor Davis is a big reason I'm now a conservative. Not just because he helped me reason out my views, but because he gave me an opportunity to actively serve our community and it changed me forever.

He had secured some funds from the city to open what we called "The Tech Center"—a modest after-school program that would offer mentoring, academic help, and internet access (this was in the early 2000s, before every household had a laptop at home and computer in every pocket) to students from across the city. The program would be free for all, and he was able to secure a reasonable contract with a cutting-edge educational software company that would install tutoring software on all of our donated computers.

I was a young mother and deeply engrossed in being a stay-at-home mom to my son, but Dad must have sensed I wasn't completely sold on that being my only vocation. He talked me into becoming the director for this new non-profit endeavor. We made an arrangement that would still allow me to spend the bulk of my hours parenting. My mother-in-law, a gracious and beautiful woman named Faith, would care for my son when he wasn't in pre-school (where she was the principal), and I would pick him up from her care every day when I was finished with work. She was excited to be grandmothering, and I was excited to have a break from mothering. Or at least that type of mothering. I quickly learned that in a situation like our after-school program, mothering was just another part of the job description. To this day I refer to those students as "my kids."

It was a win-win. I went to work with some training in charity and management, but mostly making it up as I went along. It was here I encountered the reality of my politics. I became an advocate in the public schools for parents and grandparents (we had a large number of grandparents who were raising their grandchildren). I found myself talking with teachers and principals and guidance counselors very often and

I was in and out of school buildings across the city. What I saw was devastating.

Burned-out teachers, unchecked violence, schools without air conditioning on 100-degree days, classrooms without textbooks, an apathetic parent base and shockingly dismissive administration. The problems were piled all the way to the ceiling but at the bottom of that pile were the children.

I became aware of what my public school kids were dealing with at home. I knew who was depending on welfare (most of them) and who didn't have a relationship with their father (most of them) and who couldn't read at grade level (most of them) and whose parents were struggling with making ends meet, healthcare and parenting assistance (most of them). I was in one of the most liberal cities in America, a mostly Black city that voted faithfully for Democrats for decades. Besides my father-in-law, there was nary a Republican to be found within city limits. The mayor, the city council, the comptroller, the dog catcher . . . they were all Democrats. They held all the power. We should have been living in a Black paradise. What I saw around me was pure hell for too many people.

When I approached our representatives throughout my tenure for help, or with ideas to benefit the community or in particular, provide for children and families, I was always met with the same mantra. "We don't have the money." But I knew the money was changing hands behind the scenes for so many reasons, between just about anyone in government, and it turned my stomach. We were supposed to be on the same side, but they treated me and my kids like the enemy because we weren't in their inner circle.

So, there I was, a faithful Democrat, looking at my city, my kids, my program. I got to see how all of these policies I'd supported my entire adult life worked, and I was saddened and not a little bit angry, to discover they didn't. Republicans had no hand whatsoever in the development of Gary, and yet I was looking at a city mired in failure.

When charter schools began creeping into the city, they brought a sense of hope with them. Parents were abuzz when they would come into the Tech Center to pick up their kids. They weren't sure exactly what a charter school was, but they believed them to be close to a private school, and any school that wasn't the public school they were trapped in had to be better. We were honored to host the lottery process for one of the new charters at the Tech Center.

For those who may not know, the charter school lottery system is just like what it sounds like. The names of all the applicants go into a virtual hat and students are chosen at random for submission. They had to go with a lottery system in that first year. There were just a few hundred spots and well over a thousand applicants.

Every day I would have a parent or grandparent pull me aside and quiz me about the lottery. Could I put in a good word? Could I get their name up front? Most people wouldn't hear of it when I would tell them I was just a glorified building manager for the lottery. I had no connection whatsoever to the charter school. They were just using our building. It didn't matter. The stakes were too high. Most of them were just taking every shot they could.

The lottery was held over two nights—two devastating, soul-crushing nights.

It was certainly a wonderful experience for the students who were selected for the program. Many families left happy and grateful. For my part, I was not prepared for the despair and the devastation of the parents who did not make the cut. After the first night's drawing, a distraught grandmother of one of my students approached me. She was beside herself. Her eyes welled up with tears. Her grandson had not made the lottery.

"Please, Ms. Kira," she said, voice strained. "Isn't there anything you can do for my grandson? Can you pull any strings? This is our last chance . . . my grandson's last chance."

I will never, ever forget the sense of impotence and helplessness that washed over me. Of course, I had no authority in the matter whatsoever. She was grasping at straws. That's what you do when you sense defeat. I didn't buy into the notion this would be her grandson's only chance for success, but I knew it would be more difficult. I certainly did understand why she and so many others believed that. For decades we have been stressing higher education as the key to opportunity—as the sole key, in fact. Even so, Black students have been left behind by the public system since its inception. It was a conundrum. If the only way to prosperity is higher education, but the feeder system is so broken it is hurting Black students instead of helping them, how are Black students supposed to access elite education? The only way people at ground-level can see that happening is to escape. The charter schools represented an escape, but the route was too narrow. It couldn't accommodate everyone.

There I was, watching this beautiful, devoted, distressed grandmother sob as she wondered aloud what her grandson's future would look like without access to a good school, and all I could give her was a shrug.

That was it. That was the very moment the lightbulb came on. When I looked around at what my students and their parents and grandparents were being forced to deal with in public school on a daily basis, I wondered what good it was doing to keep them trapped in their zip codes. The White kids in the suburban schools didn't worry about air conditioning or textbooks or gang activity. They went to school to learn and were rewarded for that.

Every year we in the education industry would complain about the stunning lack of resources in our local public schools. Every year our politicians and teachers unions would tell us we just need one more cash infusion, one more tax, one more bundle of federal funding and we could fix everything. And every year, the situation worsened. I mean that. At no point in my life in that city did the public schools improve. At every point, they got worse. In every, single way.

My clients and students were told by the White and Black elites in public education that they just needed to be patient, needed to advocate for more funding, needed to give them time to overhaul the system. Looking at this grandmother in front of me I thought, *Why should Black children be the guinea pigs while teachers unions and school districts take decades to reach that magical, elusive number that will finally fix everything?*

I had heard about school choice at that point, and my father-in-law had been encouraging me to become more involved in advocacy. School choice suddenly made all the sense in the world. I had been wrong about the virtues of the public-school monopoly. I could see that now. What else was I wrong about? I am a conservative to this day because of school choice, because of Gary, Indiana, because of that weeping grandmother whose most important goal was securing a stable future for her grandson. I am a conservative because I love Black people.

In Gary, trapped parents were left with only two real choices—stay trapped, or scrape together enough money to move to a better zip code for a better school. One left them with a bleak present, the other with a bleak bank account.

I am often asked about systemic racism—do I believe it exists? Many conservatives will tell you it doesn't, and that is a liberal term that just means "Everything I don't like racist." I disagree. The Cambridge Dictionary defines "systemic racism" as:

> Policies and practices that exist throughout a whole society or organization, and that result in and support a continued unfair advantage to some people and unfair or harmful treatment of others based on race.[1]

If that is the definition we are abiding by, I can see no better example of systemic racism than the current iteration of our public school system. It's a SYSTEM and a STRUCTURE that has establish EXPECTATIONS based on the UNEQUAL TREATMENT of a particular ethnic group. Progressives love to point to *Brown v. Board of Education* as a reason we need government to intervene in social affairs. They consistently neglect to mention that *Brown v. Board of*

Education was needed *because* of government policy. It is the most basic proof of systemic racism. The public education system was literally designed to push out Black students and segregate them in quality and location. So much so that citizens had to go all the way to the Supreme Court to nullify that system.

They succeeded in legal desegregation, but organic segregation is still very real and very much alive. When you purposefully design a school system that funds education based on the tax base, and then you engage in racial policies like redlining and infrastructure isolation (running freeways through poor communities, effectively cutting them off from easy access to other neighborhoods), you (again, purposefully) drive out high-income taxpayers and leave the low-income taxpayers stranded in a community that now has lost all of its funding base. It necessarily creates segregation by income level, which will always mean segregation by race.

Systemic.

I do not believe it is an accident. If conservatives are skeptical of systemic racism, don't be. It exists, but it exists in the very institutions progressive elitists insist we be monopolized by. I see no reason to beg the very people who instituted a racist system to now suddenly fix that racist system.

This is where we might take a page out of the Black Lives Matter manifesto. You can't depend on the people who broke the system to fix the system. It is my opinion we need to completely transform the system. We need to completely rethink the system.

Ask any parent who hasn't yet figured out a way to pay for private school if they would like to be able to choose the school their child attends without finances being a consideration. Anecdotally, I have yet to meet a parent who tells me they'd choose their public school over a private or charter of their choice. Even the parents in great school districts. I bet you could tell me the same anecdotes.

I live in a district with a very high-achieving public school system. We have great facilities, award-winning teachers, an exciting array of opportunities, activities and some of the best teachers in the state. It doesn't get much better for public education than where we are now. Even so, I am willing to bet you'd find nary a parent who already doesn't have a private school in mind they would transfer their child to if the money suddenly showed up on their doorstep. If even the richest schools would still lose students to choice, that's a terrible indictment of the entire system.

Some homeowners even voluntarily pay an extra property tax (called a Mello-Roos tax) to ensure even higher funding for our schools. The difference between this school district in my posh Orange County suburb and the one we escaped in the inner city of Gary, Indiana, is shocking.

We have the money in my area to mitigate the red tape and obstacles put forward by public school administrators and the state monopoly. When activities are defunded, we have the financial base to pick up the slack. When the school or classrooms need things, we can step up to provide them. When teachers perform poorly, parents force them out of the school. You can't have some jackass teacher ruining your kid's chance to get into Stanford. It's serious business. That's a luxury, and it still indicates a gaping hole in the public system. The gaps can be covered by wealthy parents. What happens when no one around has any wealth to speak of, and when a quarter of those people are dependent on government to survive?

I can tell you what happens because I've seen it firsthand. The students suffer, and the job of holding it all together falls to the very few middle-class families who can manage it, and those people often burn out quickly.

The world we left and the world we moved to were as far apart as two worlds can be. It makes it easier to understand why wealthy White progressives are often so opposed to school choice. They think every school is like their neighborhood school, which seems fine enough to them. Sure, they don't send their own kids there, but if they had to, it would be fine. They don't see the stark differences, the leaky ceilings, the burned-out teachers, the broken glass on the playgrounds, and the disintegrating air conditioning units. They don't live in a community in which hope is a scarce commodity. To them it seems totally natural the answer to a struggling school is simply to come up with some money. After all, that's what they do.

They don't see the system is broken. They can paper up the cracks with dollar bills before they even realize they're doing it.

But what, exactly, does more money get you in America's public school system? Let's take a look at some of the least and most funded districts in the nation and compare them against proficiency rates. These statistics have been culled from *Publicschoolreview.com*—a great site that offers easily digestible data, for those of us who don't enjoy spending a lot of time with math—both from their data on average spending per student and their data on proficiency rates per state.

- Utah has the lowest funding per student at a mere $8,830 per year. Math proficiency for Utah students is 45% and reading proficiency is 47%.
- New York has the highest funding per student at a whopping $38,270 per year. Math proficiency for New York students is 55% and reading proficiency is 54%.
- Wyoming's funding per student is $25,795, with math proficiency at 51% and reading at 56%.
- Texas's funding per student is $12,640, with math proficiency at 51% and reading at 47%.
- North Carolina's funding per student is $9,637, with math proficiency at 42% and reading at 46%.
- The District of Columbia's funding per student is $26,402, with math proficiency at 32% and reading at 38%.[2]

Are you starting to get the picture here? These statistics are astonishing. It doesn't seem to matter the amount of money states spend on public students; the results are tragic. This is the wealthiest, greatest country in the world, and most of our public school students—no matter the funding level—can't seem to climb above 60% proficiency. In fact, this same spending review indicates only three states have been able to break the 60% ceiling when it comes to public school proficiency—Iowa, Ohio, and Virginia. All of those states spend roughly half of what New York spends.

The system is broken. Big money, small money, more money . . . money is clearly not the issue here and we need to stop allowing Big Unions to lie to us. The proof is in the pudding. They don't know what they're doing.

YOUR NEIGHBORHOOD IS NOT YOUR VALUE

It's a cliché in the world of school choice by now, but why should a child's zip code determine their education? Why does the quality of your child's education depend on what circumstances she was born into?

The answer, of course, is systemic racism embedded in public schooling. It's a talking point my left-wing friends readily agree with. They often express surprise to hear me "admit" systemic racism is real. It's funny our commonalities end at racism. When it comes to totally dismantling the criminal justice system to rebuild it from scratch, consequences be damned, they're all for it. When I suggest we have to dismantle public school and reimagine education from the bottom all the way to the top, they act as though I suggested turning off the moon. They insist the only way to fix the system is to infuse it with more money and create more bureaucrats.

It is a nasty contradiction to suggest the entire American system suffers embedded racism and class bigotry and then demand the system fix itself.

School choice opponents like to couch the subject as an attempt to "defund the system." I'm not against completely defunding the system, but that's not the issue here. Anti-choicers can never seem to answer exactly why it is letting the money follow the children to the school of their choice would result in defunding the system. Some are simply truly ignorant of how schools are funded and don't really know how a system of choice would defund the public schools, they're just sure that it would. However, many others know the answer and it is the one thing they can't admit or they lose the argument immediately. Giving parents a choice of where to send their children might effectively defund public schools because public schools are failing. Even the ones who are successful often pale in comparison to other private or charter programs. How many parents *wouldn't* choose to send their child to a high-end private or charter school if they had the money?

Not too many.

IT'S NOT JUST ABOUT ACADEMICS

Think about all of the factors that go into choosing a career and/or finding work. Most of us find our work and career paths through the people we know and socialize with. In a 2016 LinkedIn survey, 85% of respondents revealed they found their current employment through networking channels.[3]

Your zip code doesn't just give you access to better resources, it gives you access to better connections. It gives you access to opportunity through networking. It gives you access to culture and experiences.

Our lovely little California suburb is mightily expensive. We can't afford the prestigious schools for our children. We're not the prestigious type anyway. My husband and I sacrifice a lot on this end, in the hopes the other end will have a door to the types of opportunities that come with living alongside influential people. It's not about hobnobbing, it's about access.

Our children go to school with the sons and daughters of wealthy investors, Hollywood producers and actors, musicians, and tech entrepreneurs. We may not have been able to afford all the best vacations or experiences, but they've grown up with friends who can. They've traveled and learned new things and had unique adventures as tag-alongs with their social groups. They've secured summer jobs through the parents of their friends. They've built reputations as agreeable, hard-working, interesting, dependable kids.

As they move forward into the job markets, they move forward with connections and networks. Some they'll use right away. Others may come back into their lives down the road. Always they will be known by the people who have work to offer and experiences to share.

Now imagine a child who grows up in a neighborhood where a significant portion of families are on public assistance, unemployment is high, and resources are scarce. The schools graduate barely half of their students, crime is rampant, and opportunity is low. Who is the network for those children? How many of the people in their communities go on to own businesses, to amass wealth? While the girl socializing with middle class families gets to tag along on ski trips or resort vacations, who does the little girl in the inner city socialize with? Which girl has more access, both in the long-term and in the moment?

Your network is every bit as valuable as the quality of your education. Perhaps in many cases, even more so.

School choice grants access to the corners of society some children would never otherwise find the opportunity to observe. It puts them in contact with the people who will go on to make them business partners or trusted employees. It puts them in contact with a wider world.

I had a friend who spent her entire youth in a poor, Los Angeles environ. She lived just a few miles from the beach, an hour from Disneyland, two hours from ski resorts, and a bus ride away from Hollywood. And yet, she told me she did not leave the two square miles of her neighborhood until she was eighteen. She told me once or twice she may have traveled a bit north of the city to see family or to shop, but that was about it. Her whole life was in those same blocks of concrete. It wasn't until she met her now-husband that she ventured out, and she was shocked to discover a big world around her. She went on to revel in the discovery, and to this day is a person who seeks out adventure and new experiences.

It took someone with access to introduce her to the concept of "more."

That's what our kids need. They need more. You can pour all the money you want into a failing public school. If it's in a failing zip code, the troubles will be more than cash can fix. Your network is one of the most valuable assets you have. Strong networks build strong careers. If you can build a strong network, the zip codes become far less meaningful.

But there are even more reasons to stand up for school choice, and they have been laid bare by a pandemic that brought out the worst in the power brokers and in average Americans.

MORE THAN EVER, PARENTS NEED OPTIONS

COVID-19 struck at time of sensational political upheaval, and thus our view of the pandemic was doomed from the start to be soaked in politics. The stench permeated everything. A contentious election and bitter aftermath had already left many Americans steeped in nervousness and outrage. An economy in freefall left many wondering how they would continue providing for their families. Parents, already angry at the descending chaos, were now served insult with their injury. Their children were thrown into educational stasis with no answers as to when it might end. Zoom became a multi-billion-dollar company overnight, forever earning its place in the cultural lexicon as a verb, comfortably next to Google and Band-Aid.

For some children, the educational losses, while terrible, could be eventually mitigated by time. The younger students at least have years ahead of a (hopefully) normalized education experience. For others, like my son, the losses were much more permanent. A graduate of 2020, my son didn't get to experience the All-American rite of passage of graduation. His senior year experience ended unceremoniously. One day he was at school and the next he wasn't. No prom. No activities. No school plays. No barbershop quartet state finals. No senior skip day or whatever silly thing kids do these days. It was just gone. Instead of doing everything they could to get people back to work and kids back to school, the teachers unions worked diligently to keep schools closed. Even in the face of convincing data that children were not effective carriers of COVID, and schools represent an extremely low risk as far as transmission sites go. That COVID has largely spared our children is a small miracle, and yet here we were treating them as though they incurred the same risks as senior adults with comorbidities.

I remember when my husband and I realized our baby was going to be a 2020 graduate. We thought it was so cool. It seemed so far away at the time. Surely that would be a huge milestone year. Graduations and celebrations would probably be embellished. There's something exciting about starting a new decade with an important transition. Maybe we'd finally even have our flying cars by then. Who could have imagined how terrifically off base our predictions would turn out to be?

As it turned out, 2020 was the biggest sad trombone in recent history.

Watching our children languish in isolation was devastating, but it was also enlightening. For decades parents, for the most part, have coasted along in public education, assuming their elected boards and teachers unions were working diligently on behalf of their children, preparing them for a successful future.

Parents had a lot of grace for overwhelmed teachers learning an entirely new teaching platform and for administrators trying to make sense of health data, risks, and state procedures. We waited out the spring semester of 2020, confident everyone would be back in school for the fall. Unfortunately, it did not come so smoothly. The summer brought rumblings of continued closures for the fall semester, and frustrated parents began to get nervous . . . and annoyed. The data on school transmissions was holding steady at low rates. With vaccines on the way, why were teachers unions fighting reopening so adamantly? Couldn't they see the damage building up in our children?

My final splash of cold water came at the end of that summer, when my husband and I were out for brunch one morning (dining outside, of course) and I couldn't help but eavesdrop on a couple at the next table. They were young—perhaps early thirties—and from the parts I could pick up during their conversation, it sounded like they were both teachers. They were discussing the possibility of starting the new semester back in Zoom school. I got the sense the young woman was hoping to be back in the classroom in person, but she would understand if the district chose to keep everyone home for a few more months.

"I don't mind Zoom school," she said, with a tinge of annoyance. "But I just don't think parents should be able to watch me teach. I feel uncomfortable with parents being able to see what I'm teaching and what we're doing. Because, you know, you know how some people get these days."

My jaw dropped, and I poised myself to fling myself from my chair, throw over the young couple's table with righteous indignation, and deliver a rousing, impassioned monologue about their selfishness and arrogance. It was going to be a real humdinger. I'm positive of that.

My husband, whose reflexes have come to adjust to my sudden bouts of righteous indignation over the years, caught me before I could even drop my fork. He reminded me we were out to enjoy the day and each other, and this was not the time to put a perfect stranger in their place for something they said in a conversation to which I was not invited.

I held my tongue, but that was the moment the final layers of the onion were peeled off for me. These people in public education—represented by this young couple—were so haughty, they believed their biggest obstacle in trying to educate during the pandemic was parents, not the virus that shut down society. Even though they despised the thought of parents getting an up-close peek into the classroom, they still advocated for keeping schools closed.

That has turned out to be their greatest mistake, and the greatest case for school choice to ever come along.

What we parents saw, we did not like. We were wrong to suppose our elected officials were doing the jobs we appointed them to do. We were wrong to suppose the people on our school boards were just like us, and the teachers unions were telling the truth when they said they had the best interests of students in mind, always. We saw our children were barely proficient in a lot of areas. I had to quickly teach my teenage daughter phonetics in order properly help her with her spelling and grammar studies. I know I wasn't the only one. It was eye opening.

We saw too many teachers emphasize social lessons over basic skills. We saw classroom discussions centered around sexuality, and classroom exercises centered around shaming some students for their race.

Then, to add insult to injury (there were a lot of insults being added to a lot of injuries during this time), as parents were heading back to work, teachers unions were still fighting to keep schools closed. For some families, the choices were gut-wrenching. Lose work to stay home or go to work and leave children home alone all day.

I know of several people who had to leave children as young as five home alone all day. Even as the union queen herself, Randi Weingarten, president of the powerful American Teachers Federation, looked straight in the camera every day and assured America the only thing she cared about was students.

Combined with the incursion of Critical Race Theory chaos and transgender confusion into the schools, it was a perfect storm of ineptitude. COVID had burned away the shiny veneer that was keeping us all comfortable.

Suddenly parents were left to scramble for alternatives. Those who could afford to moved to private schools that didn't have mask mandates or closures. Some formed pods and some hired their own teachers. They could do that. They had the choice because they had the money. Other parents were left to wonder, *What would I be doing for my child right now if I wasn't solely dependent on public school?*

The issue over what to do with schooling through the pandemic became hotly contested. Like everything else, it ignited a lot of fury and rage and arguments. But it also made one thing clear: if we had had a system of choice in place, we could have avoided a lot of angst and vitriol. Parents (and teachers) who didn't want their children masked all day or forced into remote learning on a whim could choose to head to schools that chose to stay open, mask free, etc. Parents who feared maskless children and in-person learning could choose to be in schools with mandates and remote learning options. Everyone would have been out of each other's way and there would have been no reason to be accusing each other of wanting to murder teachers with the inconvenient breaths of their children.

There are no guarantees coming out of any of the halls of government that we will not see more sudden, disruptive, and unnecessary school closures in the future. Many American parents are already thinking ahead to the next round of overreach and they're saying to themselves, "I can decide what's safe and what's not for my child. If this happens again, I want options."

Pop star Madonna was roundly criticized for some social commentary she gave at the beginning of the pandemic. In a bizarre video, filmed while lounging in her bathtub, the Material Girl called COVID "the great equalizer" and assured everyone "we're all in this together."

The reality was, of course, that only some of us were in this together, and the rest were using their wealth and power to skirt the rules and take advantage of the unwashed masses being forced off the streets and those bothersome small business being taken out of the competitive market. The divide between the haves and the have-nots has never been wider, thanks to Madonna's supposed "great equalizer."

However, the good thing to come out of this mess was parents were finally forced to face the truth about what was being done to public schools while they've been busy going to work and baseball practices and family gatherings. We took our eye off the ball while we just went about being regular Americans, but COVID has stripped away all the facades. All the creature comforts we depended on to keep us comforted and docile were yanked away without ceremony. In the end, I believe, that will be the greatest story from this time.

COVID woke up a slumbering middle class.

WHAT CAN YOU DO?

In a world full of Randi Weingartens, be a Loudoun County parent

What parents in Loudoun County, Virginia, have done for the battle to reform education is nothing short of a miracle. Their battle against their school board and Critical Race Theory has not only been illuminating, but inspiring.

Loudoun County is one of the largest school districts in the nation, and parents have largely been at the mercy of a school board infected with the typical "inside-the-beltway" swamp monsters. When parents began to complain about disturbing Critical Race Theory exercises and curriculum in the schools, some of the board members posted the names and addresses of angry parents in a private Facebook group, and suggested they be targeted as troublemakers.[4] Loudoun County parents figured out before the rest of us did what the biggest problem in our public education system is at the moment.

Public school officials and many teachers don't see parents as partners, but as enemies. They have convinced themselves a couple of degrees and a weekly meeting make them more qualified to raise children than the parents of those children. They genuinely believe this. Like the teacher I overheard while out to eat with my husband, they see themselves as capable and parents as incapable. And when our education providers start thinking like that, it's only a matter of time before they view part of their job as working around parents as much as possible.

Thankfully, Loudoun County parents also figured out there is strength in numbers. It's taken the rest of the country a little while to catch up. As it turns out, those Virginia parents had already been engaged in a power struggle with the school board for a couple of years prior, over transgender policies, as discussed in the previous chapter. They had been laying the groundwork for quite some time, so when COVID brought the failures of public schooling and administrations into sharp focus, their angry school board meetings were naturally a lightning rod for coverage. Suddenly all eyes were on Loudoun County, and the parents did not disappoint. They gave a master class in grassroots organizing and mentoring and inspired hundreds of copycat movements across the country. From San Francisco to Idaho to Los Angeles and beyond, parent movements are actively seeking to take on the rot we've allowed to infect our school boards.

They also turned out to be the front lines of a red wave that may potentially surge in 2022 and again in 2024. Democrat Terry McAuliffe seemed like a sure win for the Virginia governor's race in 2021. Virginia is a blue state, by virtue of the fact it houses much of Washington D.C.'s swamp culture. It seemed like McAuliffe might breeze to victory but then he made what might go down as the biggest political blunder in American history, right next to the Howard Dean scream. He said, out loud, with his whole mouth and his vocal cords, in front of a crowd with ears to hear, he didn't think parents have the right to help decide what their kids learn in school.

Republican Glen Youngkin won the governorship of Virginia in the closing weeks of the race on the backs of antagonized, outraged parents. It set the tone for 2022, and as this book goes to publication, we shall see if Youngkin's win and the incredible inspiration of the Loudoun County parents will bring us a red tidal wave and help set back the incursion of altleft policies in the political and educational landscapes, at least for the time being.

Loudoun County parents are still engaged in a battle to recall the most troublesome schoolboard members and rehaul the Loudoun County School District apparatus for good.

Take their lead. Start by going to your school board meetings regularly, even the boring ones. Don't go when there's a controversy, be present and noticed. You'll be shocked to discover all the little things that skate by when they think no one is watching. I must admit I did not attend my own school board meeting regularly until the Loudoun County controversy inspired me to be more active. I live in a conservative district in California, and I assumed everyone on the board was like me. I was surprised to discover how many progressives were on our board, and how much unnecessary spending and tinkering they were doing. They could do it with impunity because largely no one showed up for the meetings unless it was a group asking for money.

It's a pain, but it's necessary. Go to your meetings. Pay attention. Maybe think about starting a blog or social media page to keep other parents informed about what is going on. When school boards know they're being watched and know parents are willing to start a recall campaign if they get out of hand, they will begin to lose their power, and that's all many of these tyrants want—a little bit of power in their small lives. Progressives in local government are often meaner and harsher than their federal counterparts. That is because for many of them this is the one bit of power they have in their lives, and it makes them feel good to wield it wildly. They are glorified parking meter maids. They have pens and forms and meeting logs, and they think that makes them better than you. It doesn't. Show up and remind them with your presence every chance you get. Remind them you are your child's first teacher, best advocate, and greatest leader. They are just the people elected to help you teach them to read and write.

Run for school board

As I said, I was highly disturbed (and embarrassingly so) to discover how many progressives were on my local school board once I started attending regularly. I had assumed my school board would be filled with people like me as this is a conservative pocket of Southern California. Of course, it wasn't. Conservatives like you and me don't think like politicians. We believe if we want change, we must argue the merits of that change, not strong arm it through backdoor legislation and secret meetings. We surely don't have much interest in running for local offices. We're busy feeding our families and running kids around to activities and running businesses. We're not the type to get out in the street for *an entire summer* and destroy communities . . . we're busy participating in community.

I get it. You're busy and you do not need one more thing to deal with. But you must understand that progressives love government. They loathe discussion (hence the censorship we'll be discussing in the next chapter) and love strong-arming. They love testing their ideas through force rather than persuasion. They are exactly the type who will move to your conservative district with no kids and run for your school board anyway. (And frankly, more people without kids should run for school board. It's your tax money too.)

Loudoun County parents gave us a blueprint for protests and recalls, but that's the hard way. If you want to safeguard your families against these institutions in the future, I'm afraid the only way to do that is to make sure you're one of the people who gets to decide the fate of your child's learning future.

I'm proud to say that as I write this book, I have decided to run for the open seat on my school board. By the time you have this book in your hand, I hope I can say that I now sit on my school board. I've taken my own advice. No more standing around, hoping smarter, better people are taking care of things. There is no cavalry coming. We are the cavalry.

Run, run, run. The next spot that opens up, run. If your reasonable, sane, non-progressive friend is running, support the campaign. Progressives have loaded up your school boards, and now look where we are. What would your district look like if every single person on your board were a professing conservative?

Make it happen and find out.

Break the unions

Maybe the greatest revelation for many Americans throughout this whole ordeal has been teachers unions are not just not doing a great job for our children, they're actively working against our children.

Led by union bigwigs like Randi Weingarten, teachers unions advocated for schools to be closed when they should have been open, ignoring the crashing mental health of our students. They held our children hostage while they negotiated for higher pay and more time off. They "consulted" with the CDC[5] on language and masking and vaccines that would support their edicts of masks and vaccines for all children. If the unions can't keep the schools in a state of emergency, they can't keep siphoning off emergency funds from the federal government.

Teachers unions have declared parents the enemy for wanting to have their children back in school and wanting to make their own decisions about mitigation efforts. As Randi Weingarten embarked on a national tour in 2021 to visit districts, hold union meetings, and lobby politicians in state and federal departments, parents watched helplessly from home. It was too dangerous for their children to go to school, but the union officials were having the time of their lives, traveling the nation.

It stung. It outraged. It should. It *is* an outrage.

As President of the American Teachers Federation, Randi Weingarten makes nearly a half a million dollars a year. I bet your left-wing friends just love to sneer at rich people who try to tell the rest of us how to live. They think they're sneering at Republicans, and that's what makes them feel good about it. The next time they do that, point them to Randi Weingarten. While lower-class, minority families were having to choose between their jobs and leaving their elementary age kids alone all day, noted Caucasian Randi Weingarten made her full salary, a half a million dollars, and traveled, partied, and largely lived her life unchanged, even as she called parents selfish for wanting schools to reopen.

Teachers unions have long been painted as advocates for students. It's partially our fault for not being more curious as a nation as to exactly what it is they do. A major clue should be the description. It's right there in the name—TEACHERS

UNIONS. We should no longer allow union representatives to dictate the conversation around schooling nor should we allow them to paint themselves as pro-student. We can get a lot further if we all go into conversations with an honest representation of our priorities. For a teachers union, the priority is teachers. That seems logical.

It is very illogical to believe an organization that has the stated purpose of advocating for employees can also properly represent customers. The General Motors union does not represent car buyers. The nurse's union does not represent patients. The teachers union does not represent students. A union will always demand more money for less work. Look at the unions around you and see when the last time was they negotiated to take on more work.

Teachers unions are the enemy, and they've declared parents their enemy because they don't like we're suddenly paying attention to their priorities.

The good news—nay, the great news—is if you are a teacher who is just as disturbed by the union advocacy as the rest of us are, you don't have to pay union dues anymore. In 2018, the Supreme Court of the United States ruled for the right to work without being forced to pay union dues to an organization that uses your dollars for political advocacy you might not support. *Janus v. AFSCME*[6] was a revolutionary ruling, which is why a lot of people still don't know about it. Teachers unions do their best to ignore or obscure the right-to-work edict. Too many teachers have no idea it exists.

If you're a teacher who has said repeatedly you don't like how your unions have been treating parents and students and you find it frustrating, please get out now. As a parent, I must be honest with you—I'm sick of hearing from teachers frustrated with union strong-arming. If you're not going to do anything about it, your complaints are meaningless at this point. Parents are standing up for our children and you're free to join us . . . literally. You can avail yourself of your constitutional right to work and stop funding the beast.

It's your choice, but if you don't draw the line here, you'll be forced to somewhere else further down the road. By then, there may be no one left to stand next to you.

Fight for choice

Write your legislators. Sign up to support groups that are advocating for school choice. Volunteer in choice programs and stay informed about choice legislation that may be weaving its way through your state government. Make yourself powerful. There is no valid moral argument against parents being able to choose where their children attend school. The only reason choice legislation fails is because unions are flush with cash to bribe their way to their agenda. Parents need to become more powerful than teachers unions. Organize letter-writing campaigns aimed at reminding your politicians who reelects them and encouraging them to support school choice initiatives. Organize protests outside your legislator's office. Organize call-in campaigns.

Look to the Loudoun County parents—organize, organize, organize. Defund the teachers unions by leaving, and fund parent "unions." Perhaps it wouldn't even be such a bad idea to organize parent unions, since that seems to be the only language these power-hungry politicians seem to speak these days.

Ask yourself and the people around you this: If you had access to twenty thousand, ten thousand, even just five thousand dollars a year for the education of your child, what could you do for them?

Whatever you come up with, nearly every person in America can agree it would be a hell of a lot better than what public education currently offers.

CHAPTER 3

CANCEL CULTURE

THE GENESIS OF THE RIDICULOUS

In September of 2019, a young man name Carson King headed out to an Iowa Hawkeyes football game with a group of friends. Like many sports fans, he brought his own sign with him, just in case the cameras happened to drift his way. But King's sign was a bit cleverer than the typical "Hi Mom" signs. His sign was asking for beer money and displayed his Venmo ID for anyone who was tickled enough to indulge his youthful request.

Busch Light supply needs replenished. Venmo [Carson King].

Simple, to the point, and the pinnacle of American college-boy antics.

And it worked. King's sign made it to the airwaves. Americans love their beer and they love audacity. King's Venmo account began pinging with small donations, but something bigger happened. Even as the game was still playing on, King's story was already going viral. The sign was an amusing symbol of the average American college male, but what King did next was anything but symbolic of his demographic. As the donations began to mount, the young Altoona, Iowa, resident began to think hundreds of dollars was a bit much for beer money. Instead of taking that money to buy a few rounds of beer for his buddies, King told his family he planned to donate the money to the University of Iowa Children's Hospital. It was a fateful decision that, in true American fashion, was marked by incredible and inspiring highs and tragically manufactured lows. It would mark a time in King's life that surely changed his trajectory forever, but it also marks the moment when Cancel Culture fully bloomed. We might say that this incident was the genesis for the current disdain so many have for the ridiculousness of Cancel Culture.

Anheuser-Busch was as impressed with King as the rest of the country and stepped in to offer a pretty amazing deal to the college kid who started out his game day just looking for beer money. They offered to match whatever he raised for the Children's Hospital, dollar for dollar. They also pledged to continue partnering with King for more charitable fundraising in the future. Venmo stepped up too, and when all was said and done the Iowa native, and his corporate partners had raised well over a million dollars for the hospital.

It was a heartwarming story of American ingenuity and generosity. Oftentimes the internet is a very mean place, but here was story that illustrated the positive aspects of internet culture. Sometimes the power of the internet can be wielded for good . . . and oh, how good was this?

The thing is, something has happened to journalism in the last twenty years or so, although it probably began even longer ago. Woodward and Bernstein inspired subsequent generations of journalists to look at themselves as investigators. Their success in helping to bring down a Republican president ushered in a new era of investigative journalism and using the fifth estate to speak truth to power.

The problem was and always has been that most people in corporate media (what others may call the mainstream or legacy media) are liberals and Democrats. In a survey from IU Bloomington titled "The American Journalist in the Digital Age,"[1] two journalism professors discovered that in 1971 polling of newsrooms revealed journalists to be pretty evenly split among ideologies. By 2013 only about 7% of journalists identified as Republicans.

Over the decades, speaking truth to power evolved into seeking to bring down any politicians the journalist class disapproved of. That mentality permeated journalism schools. The Boomer professors began seeing journalism as a type of activism and they passed on that notion to their students, who did the same for theirs and so on and so forth. With the advent of the internet, the idea of journalism as a fifth estate that reports on newsworthy events in politics and culture gave way to the idea of journalism as blatant activism. Students growing up in a culture of political correctness and heightened sensitivities traded in reporting for advocacy. It became a moral duty to eliminate those they deemed "evil" from the political playing field.

Unfortunately, Carson King found himself a sort of mile marker in the development of modern journalism. He (and many families) benefited from reporters around the country picking up his beer money activism and sharing it with millions of Americans. He also was the unwitting victim of a fifth estate that now had moved completely toward activism. In modern journalism the way to make your name is to take down a public figure. For a heartland reporter perhaps looking to get on the radar with his progressive colleagues on the coasts, the viral beer money guy was as fine a target as any. After all he was White, middle-class, privileged, and being a White boy from Iowa he's probably either conservative or conservative adjacent.

For what it's worth, I have no idea what Carson King's politics are, and I couldn't care less. Most of the instincts of the corporate media elite are tied up in political affiliations. No doubt, King seemed like an easy target, based on the assumptions of one particular reporter at the *Des Moines Register*.

A reporter named Aaron Calvin began sifting through King's social media posts. Not just one or two years back, say, maybe to the beginning of his college career. No, Mr. Calvin dug through posts until he found an "offensive" post in which

King quoted (and digitally LOLd at) distasteful jokes (by modern standards) from the Comedy Central show *Tosh 2.0*. A show, by the way, that aired all the way until 2020. The posts were made in 2012, when King was just sixteen years old.

> A routine background check of King's social media revealed two racist jokes, one comparing black mothers to gorillas and another making light of black people killed in the holocaust. The joke tweets date back to 2012, when King was a 16-year-old high school student.[2]

Pardon my English, but what the hell kind of a "routine background check" includes parsing through eight-year-old tweets made by a teenager? "Two racist jokes"? Is *that* a joke? It was not a joke. It was creepy. Two "wrongthinks" made for one giant scandal.

King issued a short, humble public apology, but the bulk of the ire from the public was directed at Calvin and his editors at the *Des Moines Register*. A young man just raised millions for sick children and for some reason the journalists at the Register found it relevant to alert the whole world to jokes King laughed at when he was a teenager.

Calvin expressed mild shock at the idea people found his social media digging more offensive than the "racist" posts, but he failed to take into account The Golden Rule—do unto others as you would have them do unto you. I would bet money almost every American would be mortified for the world to see and hear some of the things they did as teenagers. My daughter is a young high schooler. She was in elementary school less than five years ago and even she can't even bear to look at her older social media posts (which I, naturally, think are always adorable and delightful).

My point is no one gets away with a cringe-free social media history. Everyone laughed at fart jokes at some point in their lives. Some still do, but I am definitely not talking about my husband of twenty-five years. Of course not.

Calvin seemed to figure he would be hailed as a sort of
modern-day Woodward and Bernstein, but he forgot social
media timelines are a two-way street and as previously stated,
no one gets away with a cringe-free life. Others began digging
through his own timelines and wouldn't you know it? Calvin
himself had some "problematic" posts in his past.

The *Des Moines Register* editor Carol Hunter fired Calvin,
writing a lengthy apology in the paper that read as though she
typed every word through gritted teeth. She did not spare the
condescension in her closing words.

> Reasonable people can look at the same set of facts
> and disagree on what merits publication. But rest
> assured such decisions are not made lightly and are
> rooted in what we perceive as the public good.[3]

She didn't do herself or the paper any favors in trying to justify
their little social media stunt. Her apology came off as tone
deaf and resentful and, frankly, Carol Hunter should not be
working today because of her culpability in this most unprofes-
sional matter. Calvin's response was revealing. He clearly (and
in my opinion, rightfully) harbored some ill will toward his
bosses at the *Register*. In a subsequent opinion article following
his firing, Calvin claimed he never had any intention of searching for or including those posts in his profile of King. He
alleges it was his direct supervisors who asked him to perform
a routine "background" check before publication. Calvin was
probably undeserving of the backlash aimed at him, but one
gets the insinuation from his statements that it never even
occurred to him there would be one.

That's because Calvin is a liberal reporter, and thus on the
side of righteousness. And his bosses felt it was their righteous
duty to make sure a middle-class White boy didn't get too
much credit for his good works.

That's how I see it, anyway.

Hunter's explanation that the social media investigation
was just a "routine background check" has never held water

with me. A background check is for adults. King had plenty of social media documentation during his college career that spoke volumes about his attitude and character. Hunter chose to direct Calvin to do a "routine background check" on King as far back as high school. What kind of person counts jokes you told in high school as a part of a "routine background check"? What kind of person even includes "high school" on a background check?

Since the incident, many progressive celebrities and media personalities have tried to make a joke out of it, tried to suggest there is no such thing as "cancel culture." There is only "accountability" culture. They would like to frame it as just conservative hysterics, but the drama surrounding the Carson King case only served to illustrate the rot of progressive thought policing.

Americans of all stripes could get on board with canceling the "bad guys." Nazi wannabes, White supremacists, '90s ska bands—those are easy calls. Digging into the high school musings of a now-adult who raised over a million dollars for charity seemed like a bridge too far for too many—because it was.

A GOSPEL OF UNFORGIVENESS

"Accountability" has never been a favored word on the far left. Several women are still waiting for Bill Clinton to be held accountable for their abuse at his hands. Justice is still waiting for Clinton and every other perverted Jeffery Epstein customer to be held accountable for their participation in human sex trafficking. The city of New York is still waiting for Al Sharpton to be held accountable for his Tawana Brawley lies that led to increased racial animosity in the city for decades. America is still waiting for Al Gore to be held accountable for his 10,000-square-foot, energy-suck of a mansion in Tennessee as he campaigns for global citizens to lead smaller lives for the good of the planet. And we still wait for Bernie Sanders to be held accountable for owning multiple private homes even as he routinely denounces private ownership in the name of socialism. The left's heroes never have to face accountability. They don't want accountability. Accountability denotes responsibility and that's not something they're keen on either.

What they really want is punishment. Frankly, punishment is the basis for every far-left philosophy we find permeating American culture these days. Whether it's political correctness or critical race theory or gender equity, the slimy underbelly is the desire to punish those who don't toe the line on "acceptable thought/politics."

In ancient Egypt, when an unpopular pharoah or leader was overthrown, their successor would have their names erased from all records. There are influential Egyptian leaders we know nothing about save for a mention here or there in tangential texts that managed to survive. The profiles of disgraced leaders were just about completely destroyed. An afterlife could not be enjoyed if no memory of your existence remained. It was also a way to erase not only offending ideas, but the influence those ideas might have for future generations. With no recorded history, eventually it came to be these particular leaders, for all intents and purposes, never existed at all.

It is the ultimate punishment. Cancel culture seeks to do the same thing. You know the expression, "If you can't beat 'em, join 'em"? Cancel culture amends that. "If you can't beat 'em, erase 'em."

No matter how childish it looks, erase 'em.

No matter how absurd the issue, erase 'em.

No matter how logical the defense, erase 'em.

No matter how noble or honorable of a life a person has led, erase 'em.

In fact, revolutionary father Saul Alinsky himself parroted the concept in his how-to book for revolutionaries, *Rules for Radicals*: "Pick the target, freeze it, personalize it, polarize it."[4]

He recognized persuasion is the tool of reasonable men, and an effective revolution must, at some point, suspend reason in order to make room for the questionable practices that will eventually overtake any violent thought revolution. The goal is to completely marginalize the opposition.

That is why everything the left does not like is "White supremacy." That is why everyone the left doesn't like is a Nazi. That is why everyone who opposes vaccine mandates is an "antivaxxer." That is why everyone who believes in the science of biology is "transphobic."

And that is why every person who speaks reason in the face of progressive illogic is deemed problematic and beaten with the sledgehammer of cancel culture. Conservatives might not always be the most persuasive people, but our ideas are extremely persuasive. The American values of traditional family, capitalism, and individual freedoms win handily every time they are given air to breathe. There are no better ideas and to date nothing has been as successful as the American experiment. Americanism cannot be defeated in the battlefield of ideas. The next best thing is to defeat individual Americans.

It is another Alinsky tactic, and an effective one. Don't take on institutions, take on individuals.

It's exactly the tactic employed by the Church of Scientology. During their battle for tax exempt status, church president David Miscavige took to the stage at an annual gathering and explained the church's strategy for intimidating the IRS into granting them the exemption. They targeted individual agents and their families. They stalked, harassed, intimidated with frivolous lawsuits. They made life difficult for the agents handling their cases, until finally those individuals just signed off on the status, just to make it stop.

The institution of conservatism cannot be defeated. The only way to make it stop is to make you stop. You and anyone who even comes close to sounding like you. Cancel culture is a tool to silence but also to condition.

When cancel culture comes for someone on the right, or someone like Carson King, who isn't a political ideologue but fits the profile of the most hated people on the left—heterosexual, White men—it's all about marginalizing individuals they don't like. There's no need for reason. The left has even managed to cancel "both sides of the story." They've decided what is right. Giving shelter to opposing ideas is akin to White supremacy.

In accordance, anyone who looks like they might be willing to hear out the other side of the debate gets the cancel culture treatment as well. It doesn't matter if they are allies. It doesn't matter if they are devoted liberals or generous philanthropists who give to liberal causes. Not a single inch must be conceded to the talking points of the enemy. If you are not far left, then you are alt-right. It must be that way. The ideas on the right are good ideas, effective ideas. Just like Alinsky directed, individuals must be neutralized and marginalized. If you make free and open discussion evil, you make those who advocate for it into demons.

THAT'S NOT FUNNY

We could hardly mention this subject without bringing up comedian Dave Chappelle. Chappelle is the perfect example of the irrationality of Cancel Culture.

He is a success story tailor-made for left-wing social justice culture—a Black man who grew up in Washington DC, struggling to find his place in the American dream. A high school of the arts—by his own admission—probably saved him from a lifetime of struggle. He went on to become one of the most successful entertainers of all time. His show—*Chappelle's Show*—was a groundbreaking sketch comedy show that tackled racism, bigotry, and playing basketball with Prince in a way that made everyone, regardless of politics, laugh. Chappelle had to constantly fight executives to execute his vision. As a Black man in Hollywood, he found himself routinely up against the White elites in the industry, who wanted to monetize his blackness while regulating his blackness. He made history as the first man—let alone Black man—to be offered an incredible entertainment contract to continue his show. Comedy Central offered Dave Chappelle 50 million dollars to keep his show running. Chappelle—unhappy with the atmosphere and lack of creative control—walked away and disappeared into a non-celebrity life for nearly a decade. The most famous man in comedy left behind the biggest payday in his industry's history on principle.

And then he came back a decade later to completely dominate the industry he'd left behind.

It's an American success story for the ages. It's a Black American success story for the ages. Yet Chappelle is now one of the most hated men on the left. His sin? Suggesting that perhaps men can't really be women after all and laughing about it.

Chappelle is no conservative stalwart. He has no interest in being a political firebrand. He's a comedian, and a comedian's job is to make people laugh. Some comedians do it with dad jokes or impressions, some comedians use physical comedy, and some comedians—like Chappelle—use comedy and storytelling to root out our own insecurities and prejudices, which are then laid bare on the stage, naked, messy, and wholly unattractive. We are dared to laugh at each other, and we do, and then we laugh at ourselves for laughing, and then we scold ourselves and laugh some more. Good comedy is a mirror. We all know what it's like to look in the mirror and feel a bit awkward about what we see in there.

In the hierarchy of concerns, the progressive left has somehow managed to place sexual ideology above racism. It seems quite racist for anyone to be telling a successful Black man what he is and isn't allowed to say, but the success of the LGBTQ movement has been to completely erase injustice unless it also encompasses sexuality and gender. Chappelle's status as a successful Black man does not protect him from progressive wrath.

He's too smart. He's too articulate. He's too good of a storyteller. He makes salient points and worse, he does it with disarming humor. Worst of all, he sometimes—*sometimes*—utters talking points that line up with conservative talking points. That is his biggest sin, and for that, he must walk the Plank of Culture and be tossed into the Sea of Cancellation. Nothing else matters but the messaging.

ETERNAL HELL

They can't win on the ideas and they will destroy anyone, regardless of race or social status, who dares to exhibit the least amount of intellectual curiosity about the religion of progressivism. They have completely erased Chappelle's incredible journey to success. A man like him should represent exactly what they claim to be fighting for—opportunity and success for Black Americans and "people of color."

But they are not interested in anyone's success. They are only interested in demise.

The gospel of progressivism does not operate on the notion all humans are created equal. It operates on the notion that equality can only be bestowed by man, and man can only offer equality by subtraction, not addition. We must all share in the misery of perpetual struggle instead of sharing in the joy of mutual victories.

Chappelle's victory is really a victory for all Black Americans, but we are not allowed to treat it as such. He committed the cardinal sin of taking his toe off the line. He can no longer be allowed to be seen as a thinking, feeling human being. He is the enemy. Full stop.

It is the full demonization of counterculture, and reasonable people must draw the line here. For whom among us will not eventually be caught in this web of intolerance?

We on the right were caught off guard by the ferociousness hurled toward the unassuming Carson King, who was simply looking for beer money and hastily demonized by the Church of Cancel Culture. We knew cancel culture was beginning to blossom, but it was something we ridiculed. The King case was a shot across the bow. Cancel Culture is about to become "normal" culture and the goalpost will keep getting moved until we've regressed right back to the society the progressive purists claim to be working against—a society in which the "weird" is unwelcome and everyone is expected to keep up appearances for the sake of fitting in.

We are seeing this snowball down that notorious slippery slope (to mix metaphors). In just a few years we have moved from canceling "right-wing thought criminals" to canceling anyone who doesn't positively affirm progressive values.

Look at Chris Harrison, host of the long-running *The Bachelor* franchise. When a photo of a former contestant at an "Antebellum costume party" was discovered, Harrison made two fouls that cost him his career. If you search on the internet for Harrison and his "infraction," you'll have to dig very hard to discover what the actual comments were. Most publications won't even link to them. They'll be described as "racist comments," but you have to go down the link rabbit holes surprisingly far to find the quotes. Nearly to a publication, when people talk about the incident online, they simply frame it as Harrison losing his job over racist, offensive quotes. Even Harrison's apology gives the impression of something horrible and unforgiveable.

> "To the Black community, to the BIPOC commu- nity: I am so sorry. My words were harmful. I am listening, and I truly apologize for my ignorance and any pain it caused you."[5]

What were Harrison's horrific words? Did he call Rachel Lindsay, the first Black "bachelorette," whom he was podcasting with when the comments were made, the n-word? Did he make a hurtful comment about Black stereotypes or in some way suggest Black people were inferior?

None of the above. The woman in the offending photo delivered a lengthy mea culpa about participating in the photo, and begged to be forgiven, saying it was not her intention to cause harm. She took full responsibility. Harrison, the only adult in the *Bachelor* franchise, simply called for the offender to be heard. He simply asked that before people and castmates wrote her off as a worthless human being, they let her apolo- gize and hear what she had to say. When Lindsay pointed out the inappropriateness of the party theme, Harrison incurred his second infraction, the death blow to his twenty-year career. He merely suggested things have changed since the photo was taken.

For that he had to grovel at the altar of progressivism, but it didn't even matter. He was forced out anyway. His big crime was offering grace and recognizing the shifting sands of time.

Cancel culture has no room for grace. It does not accept apologies as anything other than signs of defeat. You'll notice Chris Harrison hasn't been seen or heard from again in the reality show industry, despite his lengthy apology that hit all the right buzzwords. Cancel Culture does not aim for "accountability"; it simply aims for complete compliance or complete obliteration. In the process, it suppresses not just speech, but the ability to talk about truly bad ideas, and that should terrify us all.

Several years ago, comedian Jim Norton made a prediction in a TV interview I recently rediscovered. I wasn't expecting his prophetic wisdom, but when I heard it, my heart dropped.

Norton was asked about the budding "cancel culture" way back in 2016 and asked whether or not there were some jokes that were off limits to comedians, Norton responded with this:

> "Like Matt and Trey said from 'South Park,' it's either all okay or none of it's okay. Like [you, the host] did some very funny stuff on a teapot and Hitler. It was great, but there are people who associate Hitler with some very bad stuff . . . it's like, if we go down that road of, hey, don't make fun of don't make of this, don't make fun of that, well then people have a very legit argument to go, 'Well, don't mention Hitler in any context, because it's never humorous.'"[6]

He said this four years before actress Gina Carano was fired from her popular role on Disney's *The Mandalorian* for "offensive" holocaust comments. In the same vein as the Harrison saga, you must dig a bit deeper than anyone should have to in order to find Carano's direct comments. They are simply described as "racist/bigoted comments," but few people actually print the comments.

When the scandal erupted, I assumed Carano had made some holocaust-denying comments. Not from what I knew of her (which was next to nothing at the time) but because of the way the comments were being described. They must have been truly shocking in order to get her fired from a role that was extremely popular with Disney fans.

It turned out to be opposite. Carano was actually making a very thoughtful and gracious point about how neighbors can be turned against neighbors so easily if we let ourselves be.

> "Because history is edited, most people today don't realize that to get to the point where Nazi soldiers could easily round up thousands of Jews, the government first made their own neighbors hate them simply for being Jews."[7]

Norton's prediction had come true. Carano was making a point about treating each other with kindness and she was fired for simply mentioning a terrible event as a metaphor. We have gone from punishing people for bad words to punishing people for bad ideas to punishing people for saying words that are about bad things. Carano was well on her way to becoming the next big Hollywood "it" girl. Now she's no longer welcome in the "in crowd."

In a happy footnote to Carano's story, she doesn't seem to care. Like Chappelle, she refuses to be "canceled" and is currently partnering with the budding entertainment division at Ben Shapiro's *The Daily Wire* to produce a series of films.

The hard-heartedness of cancel culture is not compatible with the flourishing of the human spirit. It is an intellectual reeducation camp. Walls are erected around the victims, and they are commanded to regurgitate the "correct" talking points until "the powers that be" deem them successfully neutralized and reeducated. Except there's never a way out. In the religion of progressivism, there is only condemnation. There is no salvation.

If I could describe the progressive religion permeating every subject in this book, it would be as "eternal hell" punctuated by seasons of penance. We can stand by as society spirals into the fiery pit of pronouns and groupthink, or we can draw our lines here and decide we will not willingly march down to eternal damnation.

WHAT CAN YOU DO?

Just say no

Like Gina Carano, like Dave Chappelle, like many others—simply refuse to be "canceled." That is probably easier said than done for the average American, who doesn't make the amounts of money high-level entertainers make. In the world of the average American, getting canceled doesn't necessarily mean sacrificing future work or not being asked back for the next season. It can often mean being walked off the job by security immediately. In many places in America—particularly in high-cost markets like California and New York—Americans live paycheck-to-paycheck, week-to-week. A disruption in just one pay cycle could spell disaster for an entire family.

So, getting canceled the for "regular Joe" certainly does come with some immediate, real-world consequences our celebrity compatriots might not have to worry about. Everyone must consider their own individual situation and weigh the risks accordingly.

If you have the will and the means, simply refuse to be canceled. Do not even recognize the attempt. More than half of the pressure of "cancel culture" comes from the internet anyway. If you live in a progressive enclave like Los Angeles, it can be a bit more complicated.

I once was worrying about a hiking trail in the foothills near our Southern California home. We'd had an unusually heavy amount of rain that spring, and my favorite path was beginning to wash out. I asked my husband, "What will happen to that path? Will the county have to come out and repair it or fill it in somehow?" and he said, "No, people will just eventually beat a new path around it."

Such a silly little exchange but it's always stuck with me. This is what we do as Americans. It is in our historical DNA. When there are obstacles in our way, we don't give up and go home. We simply beat a new path. Someone leads, others follow, and the ground eventually learns to obey our feet.

Some of you may be called to beat a new path, to march around the washed-out points of entry, to force the weeds and overgrowth in your way to bend to your will. You may have to simply make an end run around cancel culture and blaze a new trail for others behind you. I can't say what that will look like for you. Maybe it's opening your own business, making your own films, writing your own scripts, switching jobs, switching careers, or challenging a coworker for a position in leadership. Only you know your life. Our knowledge of one another, dear reader, is separated by these pages. I can only offer advice and inspiration. You are the arbiter of what is doable in your own life. Seek wisdom, good counsel, and the opinions of your family.

Make them play by their own rules

If refusing to be canceled is a choice, forcing the other side to play by their own rules is an imperative.

Progressivism is a narcissistic worldview, made worse by the inherent narcissism of the American lifestyle. Progressives don't see the very real differences in the lives of Americans across the country. They project the circumstances of their existence onto everyone else. They see life in their bubble and imagine it could be the same everywhere if everyone would just get on board with their one set of rules. Thus, as a group, they have no foresight. They cannot imagine any of the restrictions they apply to others (in order to force them into compliance) will eventually one day apply to themselves. It is a terrifically immature blind spot, but one that is quite germane to the human condition.

I don't believe most of the progressives I interact with are racist, but if they say something I know would be characterized as evil, racist, and intolerant were it coming from a conservative, I have no problems throwing down the race card. If they get caught in their own woke webs at some point and find themselves running afoul of the liberal intelligentsia, I won't find joy in them losing jobs or losing social credibility, but I will support it. Not because I want revenge, but because I understand progressives will never change this ridiculous, intolerant culture of supposed tolerance until the intolerance actually applies to them. They all think they're good, they all think they're righteous, they all think they have performed the right rituals and made the proper offerings and they are protected members of the Church of Progressivism. Every last one of them is shocked when they discover the Church rites are not permanent and must be constantly renewed in order to find acceptance. It rocks their world when they are forced to obey the rules on the field (there I go, mixing metaphors again).

Some of the most vocal conservative pundits in this day and age are comedians, media personalities, and academic superstars who were "red-pilled" (as we affectionately refer to that paradigm shift) by cancel culture. Many of them felt safe from "cancelation" because they believed it was something that only applied to the "bad guys"—and progressives can never be the bad guys. Just stop being a bad guy and you don't have to worry about cancel culture! They went on to discover it is delusional to imagine the rules and restriction they set for one group would never eventually apply to themselves. As a former liberal myself, I can attest to the fact that once one door is opened, a whole bunch of light comes streaming in. Suddenly you find yourself looking around and asking, "If I was wrong about this, what else am I wrong about?"

I maintain the quickest and most effective way to *cancel* cancel culture is simply to uphold the rules for everyone. Report the "offensive" tweets, flag "misinformation," demand penance for progressive offenders, refuse to let then fly under the radar with their intolerance. Call for their firings, ask for their content to be removed. It's not very gracious and frankly, I don't like it, but war is ugly and this is a battleground. This isn't about revenge. It's not a tit for tat. It's a defense strategy. We have the right to defend ourselves and our way of life from the culture of demonization and unforgiveness. The American Way, as it turns out, is not the default for most people. If we are not actively defending it, we find ourselves losing it. That is exactly where we are right now.

It's time to dig in.

CHAPTER 4

CORPORATE OPPRESSION

*I*t seems like a world away by this time, but the battle over election integrity laws in states like Texas and Georgia brought us a new era of corporate malfeasance, as we saw huge companies move to punish states that enacted election reform.

Both Delta and Coca-Cola issued statements denouncing Georgia politicians after they passed election reform. In Texas, American-Airlines made a rare statement accusing the Texas legislature of purposefully restricting voting rights for Black Americans. Joe Biden himself, during his slow-walk to the White House, called election integrity laws the new "Jim Crow." It was an extraordinary combination of corporate bullying and political posturing.

The anxiety was, and remains, completely theatrical. The opposition to reform was lodged on the back of the notion that 2020 election fraud was simply a myth. It has always been my opinion the pushback was Astroturf from the start. A simple reading of the legislations would have been sufficient to debunk the insanely overdramatic claims of a "new Jim Crow." In fact, the bills were so basic and sensical I dedicated two separate episodes of my podcast to reading through them line-by-line and breaking down the talking points.[1]

You can tell that the opposition to these reforms was completely for show, because of the points they chose to get stuck on. When it came the Georgia bill, Democrat activist groups could not, and still to this day cannot, stop talking about a supposed measure in the bill that makes it illegal to give food and water to people standing in a voter line. Republicans were accused of nothing short of deliberate starvation. Their accusers touted it as just another way to suppress the Black vote.

If you've ever listened to my podcast, you know what I do is take talking points and strip them of their emotional value and break them down to their logical conclusions. It's so easy to say something you think sounds good, but when you dig into them, often what you're saying isn't what you think you are saying. This "you're going to starve Black voters" hot take is the perfect example of what I endeavor to do with my podcast and all throughout my career.

The "logic" employed in this complaint is that Black voters are typically voting in city centers that often have long lines and wait times on election days. Rev. Tim McDonald of First Iconium Baptist Church in Atlanta told CNN: "You know something is wrong when you can't give grandma a bottle of water and a peanut butter and jelly sandwich."[2]

It sounds so simple and so simply cruel. Why can't you just give Grandma a sandwich?

The legislation says nothing about starving people in line. It is, in fact, aimed at curbing gift-giving in line. It's a common practice in many urban voting locations for activists to give out water, food, and other small gifts emblazoned with political messaging or the names of candidates or organizations that support candidates. It is commonly understood to be a practice of last-minute persuasion. We may think giving someone a bottle of water with Politician X's face glued to it might be meaningless, and I suspect in many cases it is just that. Most people already know who their presidential vote is being cast for before they reach the polls, but likewise most people make a lot of last-minute decisions when it comes to local candidates or measures on their ballot. Sometimes just seeing a name—for sheriff, say, or for a district judge position—is enough to get a voter to check that box once inside the voting booth. It can be hugely persuasive, which is why it's a common practice. We already have rules against wearing political propaganda like hats and shirts to the polls and handing out brochures at the polls. The food and water angle has been used as a work-around for years and the fact such a seemingly random gesture was included in election integrity legislation should be the first clue it has represented an issue for quite a while.

It's also important to note it's not a ban of food and drink. It's simply a ban on groups who wish to pass those things out within 150 feet of a polling location. There's nothing saying Grandma can't bring her own sandwich.

Let's think about that. Are we to believe Black voters are too stupid to assess a wait time when they walk out the door to head to an event? We wait in line all the time for concerts and movies and bathrooms, and no one worries about starving while we wait. We come prepared for a long wait or we simply suffer through the boredom and occasional hunger pain until we can find sustenance on our own. No one calls that a civil rights violation. We just call that reality. Lines come with lots of people. Grandma has been alive a long time, and surely knows how to prepare for the unexpected when she leaves her home. My own grandmother (may she rest in peace) had a serious Coca-Cola addiction. After decades of daily consumption, she eventually got to the place where she would start to become ill and get migraines if she didn't have enough of the sugary drink. These days, there are plenty of places to find soft drinks 24/7, but through most of her lifetime she just couldn't be sure if there would be a place open at all hours should she run out of Coke. She was always prepared when she left home, because she loathed fountain drinks. It had to come out of a glass bottle (first) or a can (second). She didn't demand anyone had Coke waiting for her when she arrived. She fully recognized where she went might not always be able to accommodate her thirst.

Granny always, always, always had a can in her purse, a six-pack in the trunk of her car, and a bottle or two in the glovebox.

One reason I left the left is because of how infantilizing their rationale can be, particularly when it comes to Black Americans. Their ideology often treats us as if we are simply incapable of rational thought or of caring for ourselves. I admit that as a liberal I too carried the same condescension. As I recounted in my chapter on education, it was when I served my community and became involved in the day-to-day lives of the people around me that my heart, and my ideology, changed.

Their solutions for us always involve making other people give us things, which in turn makes us dependent on people to give us things. They never want to empower us to provide the things. The voter ID argument is the most pathetic of these infantilizing political arguments because it requires us to suspend everything we know about identification in American society. We need it to open bank accounts, cash checks, drive, go to school, rent or buy a home, get into a bar, and sadly in many places you now even need it to enter a restaurant or an indoor event space. The progressive left asks us to pretend those are normal and acceptable requirements for participation in society, but somehow the equivalent of Jim Crow for the voting booth. They'll spend their time and money organizing transportation campaigns to help get people without vehicles to the polls, but they won't lift a finger or spend a dime to help the small percentage of Americans without government-issued ID to the DMV to apply for one.

If you sit and think about it, it's mighty suspicious. Could it be the voter ID argument is simply a talking point and not an actual issue?

Color me shocked.

It's a thread they insistently hold onto because the truth is Black people already vote and vote en masse, and we know this because Democrat activists cannot stop complaining about how Black voters saved America from Trump and got nothing for it from their Democrat overlords in return. It's a desperate attempt to continuously recall Jim Crow, even though there is not a single place in America where Black Americans are not allowed to vote, or egregiously blocked from voting. Our ancestors fought hard and spilled their own blood for this moment, and the professional agitators can't let their spirits rest in that peace. It's a slap in the face to those who risked everything to bring about what we now take for granted.

It's the "tie my shoelaces" argument for lifting all election safeguards, and it's tied (forgive the pun) directly to the infantilization of the Black American community. Progressives choose to view any basic challenge in getting to the polls as voter suppression. In the end, if someone can't come to your house, wake you up in time, fix your breakfast, tie your shoes, and drive you directly to the polls, it'll be called suppression.

Anyone who claims racism has been defeated is a solid idiot. That being said, anyone who claims Black people don't know how to pack a lunch before they leave the house is also a solid idiot.

My point in making this argument is it is precisely what the corporate bleeding hearts have not done—make an argument. They have simply licked a finger and stuck it in the air to see which way the wind is blowing. It would be mildly annoying if it were just a matter of marketing, but in an economy that is becoming increasingly hostile toward small business, corporate mergers are more and more common. That means we are seeing fewer and fewer entities owning more and more consumer real estate. Their power masses as they amalgamate and that leaves the little guy on the losing end.

Corporations like Delta and Coca-Cola provide a lot of jobs, a lot of products, and thus a lot of taxes. They use their buying and spending power to lobby and influence politicians, and when they take on a certain ideology or point of view in social issue, they can become a hammer with which to beat down the will of the people.

In 2020, Florida Governor Ron DeSantis signed a bill banning businesses and companies from instituting vaccine passports. Many in conservative intelligentsia, eager to separate themselves from the local yokels of the conservative movement, called themselves intellectually honest for advocating against DeSantis's move. The reasoning goes, if we believe in minimal government and individual rights, then we must support the right of businesses to impose mandates if that's what they wish to do.

I don't necessarily disagree and if we were living in normal times (whatever that even means these days) perhaps it would be a valid point. But what is a leader supposed to do when he recognizes Big Business is so intertwined with Big Government that it can be used to strong-arm the general public? For instance, the federal government cannot impose vaccine mandates on the entire population, but they can impose them on government workers, and they can incentivize Big Business to do the same by offering tax breaks, or even disincentivize them by denying government contracts to those without mandates. They can withhold billions in COVID funding if they choose. It's effectively a bribe. If Big Business is being used by Big Government to curtail the constitutional rights of Americans, isn't that a violation that deserves a response?

Delta, Coke, American-Airlines—they are all entities who have gotten too used to their influence and forgot about their customers. The problem with these behemoth corporations is that the millennials are now in charge, and too many millennials know nothing about capitalism and too much about social justice. Whereas in my grandmother's generation it was commonly understood the customer is always right, the customer is king, the customer is who you aim to please. The generation of her grandchildren and great-grandchildren have been baked in the notion society is there to please them, and the customer is only right as long as they're convenient. Profit isn't a motivator, but (thank you, Obama) change is.

I can already hear my hippie parents scolding me for insinuating it's bad to not care about profit.

Profit is just earning, and earning is good. Like anything, we can make it our idol and then it's dangerous. Profit is a necessary element to success and replicating that success. The millennial generation is the participation trophy generation.

Their parents still own the companies and the businesses. They themselves have never had to balance the books. They start families later into life, and so aren't sobered by the trials of supporting a family. They can elevate social causes over practicality because it costs them nothing. So now we are stuck with a bunch of people in charge who have had a delayed adulthood and have no real clue what it means to start, grow, and run a successful business empire.

It was a mystery to me for a long while as to why the older generations who still own these businesses continue to cave to the "social justice at all costs" crowd. Surely, they understand their customers are a pretty diverse bunch? Why risk alienating half of your customer base over legislation that isn't really that controversial and you haven't bothered to read anyway? Then I had a fascinating conversation with Founder and CEO of Varsity Spirit, Jeff Webb, who told me the businessmen of old were aging out of the day-to-day and the boardrooms were being occupied by millennials who hadn't built the businesses, but now were running the businesses.[3]

Webb told me today, the most powerful department in any company is human resources. The #MeToo movement and Black Lives Matter may have done good things in facilitating more discussion around harassment and discrimination, but they also unleashed a new sense of superiority in victimhood. When chained to cancel culture, it turned out to be a lethal combination. A poor quarter is no longer the worst that can happen to a corporation. Now they can be permanently damaged by one terrible accusation of sexual harassment or worse, racism. A well-timed Twitter campaign could damage their reputations for good, or least for the foreseeable future. Anti-racist trainers have become more valuable, and more influential, than business consultants within these companies.

Corporations used to be slaves to the almighty dollar, now they are slaves to the almighty Woke. It's killing freedom.

They know at the end of the day, most politicians want the tax flow, and they can use their outsized reach, coupled with an outsized sense of social responsibility, to supersede the will of the people. It has become dangerous because it is sometime effective. For a moment, it seemed as if they would succeed in tumbling the much-needed election integrity laws in Texas and Georgia. The pressure was enormous and if it succeeded in nullifying legislation in two red states, the implications for the will of the people moving forward were dark.

To the relief of many, Georgia and Texas held their ground. In particular, the Georgia Senate officially rebuked Delta Airlines, which has a hub in Atlanta, reminding them they receive billions in state subsidies every year.

Delta and Coca-Cola ended up walking back their over-reach, and the story they have to tell should lay the groundwork for how we should combat this threat of corporate/government collusion.

The 2020 elections brought into focus a new and surprising reality. Until the Trump era, Big Business was seen as an exclusively Republican villain. It remains the Republican villain in most Hollywood movies these days. The terrific irony is it is the Democrat party who have now become the party of corporate America. They are the shills, and the sellouts, and the tax evaders. They are the Darth Vaders of business, making backroom deals with corrupt politicians to maximize their profits and squash their competition—at least that's how Hollywood often depicts the corporate set. The progressive corporate world has done little to dispel the stereotype in the last few years.

Republican politicians and activists need to take advantage of this shift and adjust the message accordingly. For years, Democrats have succeeded in marketing themselves as the party of the working class, and since most Americans are working class, it has been quite successful in keeping them competitive. They've become the party of unions because unions were once the champions of the working class. Now they've become the champions of greed and the enemies of innovation, and thus the American Dream. Where unions used to be vital to the empowerment of the American worker, now they are a drain, led by bloated, overpaid bureaucrats who spend more money lobbying politicians than they do helping the very people they say they represent. At this point it's a big Ponzi scheme with the worker at the bottom and the Randi Weingartens at the top. The small business, the individual entrepreneur, the independent contractor, the mom trying to make ends meet while pursuing her dream of becoming a contractor who can stay home while she earns—the Democrats have left those people behind at the behest of the unions. Republicans need to rebrand and go get those scrappy entrepreneurs who have been abandoned. Progressives—with the help of their friends in Hollywood—managed to make corporate America very uncool. Conservatives could do the same.

WHAT CAN YOU DO?

Make noise

Eventually Coca-Cola and Delta both walked back their statements condemning the Georgia law. Major League Baseball did move their All-Star game out of Atlanta to Colorado that year, but it was not lost on fans and observers they moved thousands of jobs out of a city with one of the highest Black populations in the country, in the middle of a pandemic that had just crushed the economy. It didn't matter. Georgia stood their ground and Texas did the same and companies took a second look at their wokeness. The tide stemmed.

That's because Georgia constituents and customers from across the country spoke their mind. It may feel like you're up against a behemoth when you complain about the wokeism of certain corporations, but don't forget you represent their customer base too. It's not like Coca-Cola is a company with an ideological product—like guns or those stupid "Hate Has No Home Here" signs. They sell a broad spectrum to a broad base. It's logical to surmise their base, much like America, is pretty much split down the middle when it comes to politics. They're listening to the loudest group, not the largest group. So, get loud. Progressives are experts in making noise, and as you can see, it works.

Why can't it work for you too?

Boycott/buycott

It's a tried-and-true strategy, but boycotts are certainly still an option. This is still America. Money still talks and you represent a lot of money. In the age of corporate mergers, it's becoming more and more difficult to effectively boycott one entity. Johnson & Johnson, for instance, owns over 250 subsidiaries. That means they make a ton of the things you use every day. Often top-tier brands like that even provide the off-brand products you may purchase as a replacement; they just don't put their brand on it. Given the current consumption rates of Americans, it would be exhausting to attempt to source every single product on your shopping list all the time. More power to you if that's what you want to do.

But a boycott doesn't have to be a full stop. A "slow down" can be just as effective in hurting a bottom line. You may not find it realistic to completely abandon Amazon. After all, they do provide a good service. But perhaps you cancel your Prime membership or limit your spending and purchases to only a certain amount per month. Target has been a frequent offender in the social justice wars, but my problem is I love Target. I never did do a full-on boycott, but there's no doubt I have spent considerably less money with them since they got into the ideological arena. Scaling back from one trip a week to a few trips a year is significant. It all counts against the bottom line, so don't give yourself a hard time if you can't wean yourself off your favorite stores. Every little bit helps.

I like to "buycott." It's a lot easier and it's better for the overall economy. It feels less punishing to the good, hard workers who often get caught in boycotts as well. When I see a company standing up for the things I value, or doing good work, or resisting the "resistance," I make it a point to seek out and buy their products whenever possible. The Chic-Fil-A story is a classic example. When gay rights activists targeted CFA for their pro-traditional marriage stance, they were sure they were about to put the chicken restaurant out of business. Instead, they ended up creating one of the biggest business booms of the century so far as supporters showed up in droves to buy delicious chicken sandwiches and waffle fries—for America. The lines for CFA have never recovered and the attempted boycott is now a humungous footnote in economic history. If you're not into boycotting, buycotting sends its own message too.

Say thank you

A friend recently reminded me to do this when I shared with her my surprise that my local school board was resisting California's school vaccine mandates.

"Did you send them a thank-you note?" she asked.

I was taken aback a bit. I hadn't even thought to.

"It makes a difference to them, you know, to know you're watching and you appreciate them when they come through for you."

She was absolutely right, and now I pass on that wisdom to you. When a company or a politician gives you a win or steps up for your beliefs, consider sending an encouraging note or email thanking them for their courage. Mob culture is scary, no matter who you are. It takes a certain amount of bravery to stand against it. There's nothing wrong with recognizing bravery once in a while. They'll remember you did when the time comes again to take a stand.

CHAPTER 5

BIG TECH, BIG MEDIA, BIG PROBLEMS

O n January 6, 2021, I was in Tucson, Arizona, attending a retreat for my husband's company. It was some kind of super-duper health retreat, where they didn't use sugar, served a lot of lemon/ginger concoctions, and offered a lot of yoga. To make matters worse, alcohol was limited.

I was certainly not in my element, but the retreat provided a welcome isolation. Cell phones were not allowed in the common areas and if you needed to pull out a laptop to work, you either had to head to your room or go to one of two designated areas for electronic use. The idea was that the resort was a respite from our digital hellscape.

So imagine my shock when I returned to my room after a lovely lunch of roughage, and discovered the internet had exploded. Hundreds of thousands of people had gathered at the Capitol to protest the results of the election, and now a few hundred were pushing their way past barriers and into the Capitol. Because of my isolation, I sort of rolled my eyes but didn't take it too seriously. I knew people who were in attendance at the Capitol at that very moment. My friend, actor Nick Searcy, was in fact streaming live at that moment from the Capitol steps. There was nothing scary or chaotic going on from what I could see on his feed. It seemed like a typical conservative protest—lots of Gadsden flags and Americana. I figured a few people got out of hand and decided that after a summer of Antifa burning and looting and the press calling it peaceful, they surely had the right to check out the People's House, uninvited. They would get in trouble and the left would roll their eyes at these immature protesters.

But that's not what happened. Instead of looking at it for what it was—a protest where a few hundred people decided to get naughty—the left jumped on the opportunity to sow fear and victimhood. They labeled it an insurrection and immediately declared Donald Trump responsible. I have a close friend who told me recently he believes Donald Trump had every intention of overthrowing the United States government that day.

It made me laugh out loud. It still makes me laugh when I think about it. January 6th had become steeped in rhetoric that day and has been ever since. My friend was just repeating his fears, which are legitimate fears if all the news you consume comes from the CNN chyrons and *The Daily Show*.

It only takes a couple of seconds to ask oneself just exactly how these "insurrectionists" planned to defeat the police, let alone the United States military. How do people think America runs? What was the plan? What were the mechanics? Do we believe the United States military, the Secret Service and the National Guard just sort of go with the flow? That they swear oaths to the person who sits in the Speaker's chair or the Oval Office instead of the Constitution?

Just the thought is ludicrous. Perhaps I—and people like me—am just prone to dismiss the notion because I understand the second amendment, and why we have one. It's a bit ironic, if you ask me. Tell a progressive that the second amendment was created to protect Americans from a tyrannical government that could turn on them at any moment and they'll call you a crazy conspiracy theorist.

Tell a progressive just because 300 people got saucy at the Capitol one afternoon doesn't mean they could overthrow the entire American government, commandeer the United States military, and install Donald Trump as dictator for life and they'll call you a crazy conspiracy theorist.

Either tyranny is close at hand but for our ability to protect ourselves against it, or it's a conspiracy theory. They can't have it both ways. But of course, that is exactly what they want. They want Burger King America—have it their way.

The progressive left led by Democrats who couldn't control their excitement, looked at January 6 as an opportunity. Knowing typical low-information cable news viewers would not look much past whatever narrative they wove, the progressive left set about demonizing every single person who voted for Trump or didn't vote for Biden. This was their chance to completely ostracize half the country. Seventy-seven million people—maybe more—voted for Donald Trump. They were merely the other half of the country, but to progressives they were devils. Trump's outsider victory had rocked them to their core. How dare the American people refuse Mrs. Inevitable President herself and elect a complete outsider who hadn't been approved by the establishment of the left and/or right?

All of these factors were swirling in the background as I sipped my post-lunch lemon ginger smoothie (good for the immune system and joints, obviously) and sifted through my social media and emails. An urgent message had been posted to our work backchannels. We needed to get on a call right away.

Facebook had flagged a post from one of our writers. Our page that hosted over half a million people could possibly be suspended, taking a big chunk of traffic with it.

Suddenly I went from complacent about the situation to panicked. What I saw on the TV and what my friend Nick had been streaming hadn't given me a second's pause. I thought of it as nothing but rowdiness—an immature and dangerous rowdiness, but rowdiness nonetheless—and any logical adult would have agreed. Now the social media powers were addressing the situation as an all-out coup.

As it turned out, one of our most esteemed and experienced writers had written a stirring piece on the inevitability of a protest like the one currently occupying the nation's capital. In it, he posited a country that had grown to distrust their leadership, the press and the electoral process will naturally devolve into the disruptive chaos we were witnessing at the Capitol. When Americans have no sense of stability or trust in their government, they become ungovernable. In the post, out writer used the term "protest" and other neutral descriptions for what was happening in real time. Facebook flagged it because it didn't refer to the incident as an "insurrection." The tech overlords had deemed it akin to aiding and abetting the enemy for not referring to and/or framing the event as an insurrection. For the first time, we were being suppressed, not for using specific phrases, but for *not* using specific phrases.

My casual sense of annoyed bemusement that day (made easier by my luxurious, sugar-free isolation) shifted to a deep dread, as a new reality washed over me. The internet, once the wild-wild west when I began this journey, was no longer an open range. We had welcomed Big Tech into our lives because they made it easier to connect, more fun to connect, and changed the way we communicated. We weren't paying much attention to the power they were amassing and how much we depended on their supposedly free services, and now, suddenly they were the arbiters of free speech and expression. Suddenly, they had the power to change our words or end our livelihoods.

OUR BRAVE NEW WORLD IS HERE

The progressives in legacy media convinced themselves Donald Trump had sent a coded message to protesters to overthrow the government. Again, ignoring the logic around exactly how that would be accomplished. It didn't matter. Outraged that a man like Trump was ever given the authority by voters to step into the Oval Office, they set themselves on a narrative journey.

All they had to do was completely demonize one half of the country as domestic terrorists, their only sin being casting a vote in an election.

The following weeks were chaotic. With Trump officially out of office, his power and influence as the President of the United States was no longer a threat to Big Tech and their media cohorts. They went to work right away.

Trump was removed from every mainstream social media platform. Images and videos of him shared on YouTube and other places were flagged or outright banned. I attended the annual Conservative Action Political Conference in February of that year, where Trump spoke for the first time publicly since the election debacle. YouTube refused to simply carry the live stream of his remarks. Just think about that for one moment—a media platform refusing to air video of an outgoing American President, one of the few men living to ever hold the highest office in the land and even the world. One reason there always remains a certain amount of public respect even for the worst presidents is because we have a shared understanding at least half the country voted for this person. He speaks for and to at least that half. While not everyone may be excited to hear from Jimmy Carter, we all agree Jimmy Carter can be seen and heard by even the people who didn't vote for him. The historicity of the office demands it. This was a massive shift in post-presidential etiquette. Big Tech went full ancient Egypt on the man, doing their best to simply erase him from history, or at least to the best of their ability.

Their ability was, and remains, quite outsized.

With Trump socially immobilized, Big Tech came after his supporters, or anyone they deemed supporters. By now they had been completely infected by cancel culture parasites and began working their way down a long enemies list they'd been compiling since Trump's election. The American people had betrayed the coastal elites. They would move heaven and earth to make sure that never happened again.

Overnight, Twitter banned and suspended numerous verified (or as we call them, "blue-check") conservative accounts.

Others, they shadow-banned—a term for limiting the visibility of an account without the poster's knowledge. The poster can still post content and see their own content, but their network won't see most of it. It simply disappears into the ether.

I watched helplessly as the modest following I'd managed to amass over a decade on Twitter began to plummet—one thousand, two thousand, three thousand . . . just gone. It didn't stop until nearly 8,000 accounts had vanished from my follower count. Even then, I was unable to add to my count for months. For every 150 followers I gained, I lost the same. It was a daily occurrence. Big Tech progressives tried to tell us this was simply a bot purge—just some annual housekeeping that just happened to come after Donald Trump was effectively banned from the internet. It seemed so funny that not a single blue-check progressive account seemed to get caught up in that "bot purge." I guess Twitter robots don't care for progressive social media politics.

CNN's Jake Tapper took to Twitter to ridicule conservatives who complained (and we did complain . . . bitterly) about their crashing counts. He implied it was childish to be concerned at all: "I would tell you how many followers I lost but I have no idea what I had before because I'm an adult."[1]

He had over 3 million followers . . . in case you were wondering.

Tapper was being intentionally obtuse. Of course, it's not about a popularity contest. To be upset over that certainly would be childish. The real problem with the purges and the shadow-banning—besides the fact it seems pretty one-sided—is that your follower count is your reach. By suppressing conservative accounts, Twitter was suppressing conservative reach. They knew exactly what they were doing and, in my opinion, so did Tapper. He was just being saucy because he knew his own intentional suppression of newsworthy but damaging stories about Biden and other Democrats had helped take the election out of Trump's hands. Call it what you will—I call it gloating. I'm sure Tapper would too. I can't even be mad at him for it. It was a Herculean effort I'll discuss a little later in this chapter. He was rolling in the glory of the fruits of his labor. Fair enough.

For the unwashed Twitter masses, however, it was a chilling sign of things to come. It was not just a purge of followers, but a purge of thought. Social media had become a place for us to share our thoughts. What happens when the place where everyone goes to chat starts giving people a list of things they can't chat about at the door?

Social media also launched the era of fact checkers, and that's where things truly met a dangerous nexus.

This story of Big Tech censorship and what it will do to the future if we allow it to continue, cannot be told without talking about the agenda of Big Media in tandem. Big Tech and Big Media have combined to make themselves one giant, influential force. I'll combine them here too, just to make it a bit easier on all of us. BigTechMedia is born.

In the lead-up to the elections, we saw legacy media outlets refuse to cover negative stories about Democrats, including a verifiable scandal involving walking caricature of an entitled, neglected, rich boy—Hunter Biden—and a secret laptop containing state secrets.

There was a coordinated effort between Big Tech, Big Media, and Big Government to defeat Donald Trump. It was perhaps the most pernicious, widely coordinated campaign in history. It marshaled the power of censorship, legislation, and story suppression to give the weakest candidate in modern memory and the weakest vice-presidential candidate in modern memory the best chance to come out on top; and come out on top they did, in a result still questioned by many to this day.

For months we couldn't publish or record any sentiment that definitively labeled the election "stolen." This went for most conservatives. We had to use neutral language at the least, and in some cases the only acceptable language when writing on the Capitol incident to get past the Facebook censors was to label it an "insurrection." Even to use the word "protest" would flag some content in conservative media. I began playing with words—I refused to bow to the term "insurrection" to describe a few hundred weirdos armed with water bottles waltzing into the Capitol Rotunda. I would use terms like "the incident at the Capitol" or "the kerfuffle" or "the events." I absolutely refused, and still to this day, to use "insurrection" at the barrel of a gun held by liberal censors, aimed at my employment. I don't consider it one and I won't lie to please a faceless corporate drone sitting at a desk in some coastal bubble he's fashioned for himself out of lies and gluten-free croissants.

It was very serious. Using "unapproved language" could result in our social media pages being removed either permanently or temporarily (and we never knew which one would be the outcome; these things happened without warning or notice).

Accounts were muted or suspended, YouTube channels were wiped out, livelihoods were erased in seconds if one ran afoul of the social media censors. We were forced to comb over every article submission multiple times, send it through multiple internal administrators and fact checkers. In what I consider to be an ironic twist, mainstream right-wing media became and remains the most factual news media. Outlets like mine were forced to back even simple opinion pieces, and we all became adept at sourcing liberal outlets and liberal-friendly information centers. Entities like Twitter and Facebook have an appeals process through which you can contest a flag on content or a suspension. Part of the process is being able to prove what you said is true, so we learned quickly we had a better chance of winning appeals if we made sure to source everything from liberal-friendly corners. We dared them flag their own facts. Sometimes we won, sometimes we lost. All along the way we were balancing on a frightening tightrope. Our readers, and in my case even many of our writers, did not understand the battle being waged behind the scenes to simply keep our publications alive. In our frantic January work calls, we spent a lot of time mulling over how much we could say publicly about what was going on. We needed to let the dust settle before we could make definitive plans about how best to combat the censorship. Some felt we were acquiescing, but I knew we were just trying to keep everyone employed until we could come up with a workable strategy.

Through it all I watched with increasing frustration as my progressive liberal friends and family not only took on full (and frankly overwrought) hysterics regarding the unfolding events, but also cheered on blatant censorship. The progressive mindset is geared toward groupthink. I know this as a former liberal—though probably not progressive—myself. Because modern progressives often gauge their political values based on how many people agree with them, they find it impossible to separate wheat from chafe. For them everything in life is an all-or-nothing scenario. It's a type of projection. They believed if there were a few hundred Americans willing to be ushered into the Capitol for some shenanigans, they could only have come to that conclusion by being influenced by someone or something. They had the wrong information, bad information. If only that information could be controlled, so could the wrong decisions of those very bad, dumb Americans.

I tried to explain to the friends I thought to be more reasonable about the issue, that censorship is not a nuanced concept. What they were calling for was the elimination of an entire thought structure, one that I employ and that employs me. They did not have access to what was happening behind the scenes. They could not see the completely irrational lengths we were being forced to go to just to maintain employment, while our liberal counterparts were (and still are) able to say whatever they wanted and make any accusations they wanted without repercussions. A two-tier system of information segregation was forming and they were cheering it on.

The thing is, censorship never works the way you think it will. It never stops where you think it should. No tyranny does. My friends on social media were inclined to poo-poo my complaints and my pleas for them to stop supporting the elimination of free expression, that it was dangerous to do so.

"Oh we're not talking about people like you, Kira. You're one of the 'good' ones. We just mean crazy insurrectionists."

What they failed to understand—perhaps even on purpose—was I was being labeled an "insurrectionist" simply for being a conservative writer. I didn't support the Capitol rioters; I still don't support disrespecting hallowed historical and federal grounds just to make a point. I didn't support it when Black Lives Matter was burning down churches and I didn't support it when people put their feet up on Nancy Pelosi's desk and took selfies.

Still, my work was being subjected to Orwellian levels of censorship and my friends cheered, telling me I was just exaggerating the situation. They still don't believe the gravity of what was happening. They still dismiss it as conservative whining.

The incurious callousness which with people I respected treated the rising censorship was too much for me. I went from being a daily poster on Facebook to simply exiting. I couldn't stand the smug posts of friends and acquaintances who really imagined they were on the side of righteousness by demanding we police free speech. They didn't care that the net they enjoyed seeing set was coming for people like me too, not just the fringe weirdos. They didn't care at all and that hurt.

I don't think it's healthy for us to see every thought of the people we love. It can create resentment, and I was seething at resentment for people I had thought at least fair-minded. So I left them to their Facebooking and decided it would be better for all of us if I fought this battle outside their peripheral vision. They could keep thinking censorship and fascistic policy won't swallow us all, and I could keep thinking maybe they were somewhat reasonable people who just have different political views than myself, and who maybe spent a bit too much time getting their news from cable news chyrons and headlines shared on social media.

But that's the thing about bondage. If we allow it to come for one, it will eventually come for all. This is the genius of our Constitution, when employed faithfully. It is a numeration of limitations on government, not people. Trying to control human nature is a fool's errand. Unfortunately, we are ruled by fools and foolishness. They believe that limiting human nature can bring peace.

It's such a childish way to think, which is why for them the solutions to competing ideas always involve ruling over someone instead of persuasion. Their big idea to make everyone think the way they do is to put their hands over their ears and shut their eyes and yell "lalalala I can't hear you!" Which would be fine if that's where it ended; but these people want to get rid of half of us. I know people who call themselves kind, reasonable, tolerant, and "inclusive" who are literally hoping half the country dies. You don't even have to take my anecdote seriously. You can just log into Twitter on any given day and see a litany of posts practically begging for the genocide of people who voted for Trump or reject overreaching health mandates. It's terrifying.

It is the future of discourse if we don't demand that reason be applied right now. In fact, while I always default to grace, there comes a time when grace should not be left to stand alone. When bad ideas turn to evil ideas, we cannot simply depend on "live and let live" and hope our elected officials do what it right. How do you know an evil idea? Any idea that proposes the solution to ideological differences is to segregate, separate, punish, and even disappear a group of people based on their politics is an evil idea.

The progressive left cannot cope with the free exchange of ideas for several reasons, one being they cannot defend their ideas effectively. That's why so many exchanges become so contentious. The progressives who can defend their ideas aren't progressives at all, they are liberals and that we can work with. We cannot work with a wholly unreasonable subset of people who insist any idea that contradicts their own is tantamount to terrorism.

Their argument has become free expression encourages lunacy if not monitored and shaped by those in a higher position. Perhaps there is some truth to that argument, insomuch as everyone is inspired by something. I hope to inspire you to action with this book, but it is not I who decides for you if you will do something or not, act or not. That is your prerogative. That has to be *the* prerogative. It is a dangerous path to insist that forcing people to think the same way and vote the same way is the only way to peace. It is, in fact, the surest way to oppression. That is why the Constitution leaves these decisions in your hands, not the hands of your government.

If we allow this notion to stand, we are condemning ourselves and our children to a bleak future. It isn't simply a matter of standing up for our beliefs and being heard. The progressive left is actively shutting down the channels through which we can be heard. We saw the brutal beginnings of this prior to the election, we suffered the first wave of enforcement after January of 2020, and we now remain embroiled in a battle for the spirit of freedom itself.

Big Tech has combined forces with Big Media to create a chilling atmosphere of censorship and if we don't fight back now, we will find ourselves in a situation where we will have no ability to fight back at all.

FREEDOM IS DANGEROUS TO BAD IDEAS

These people aren't just seeking to squash our voices, they are seeking to change the reality of information completely. We can scream all we want about COVID studies that prove mask mandates are pointless and COVID vaccines have limited effectiveness, but if we can't share the information or comment on the information in what has now become the equivalent of the public square—that is social media—then does that information even really exist?

They are changing socially agreed-upon definitions right under out feet. They seek to change the definition of our rationale.

Just look at the nefarious efforts to malign Americans who want to remain free of government coercion when it comes to COVID vaccines. In September of 2021, Merriam-Webster Dictionary changed their definition of *anti-vaxxer*. The accepted definition has been, until this moment in time, a description of people who are opposed to vaccines. On September 29, 2021, Merriam-webster updated their definition to include people who are opposed to mandates.

> A person who opposes the use of vaccines or regulation mandating vaccinations.[2]

For contrast, Dictionary.com still uses the widely accepted (currently) definition.

> Of, relating to, or noting people, especially parents of young children, who distrust or are against vaccination.[3]

"Orwellian" is a term that has become all too common these days, but there is no better way to describe this deliberate moving of goalposts. We can take our toys and go home but doing that only emboldens them. If we don't draw our lines here, and demand our politicians draw lines, then we are ceding control of the flow of information to hostile actors. Those who control information control the truth. It is the truth that makes us free, which is exactly why they want to be the only arbiters. Freedom is dangerous to bad ideas.

This is why we need to be fighting for even the worst thinkers among us to be able to express their terrible ideas. Neuroscientist Dr. Jordan Peterson often says you can't respond to a bad idea you can't hear. There's no good argument for censoring bad ideas. Every argument immediately descends into oppression. There is no good example of a society that suppresses opinion that does not end up suppressing their entire population. The answer to bad speech is more speech. It's a cliché but it's true.

Progressives in Big TechMedia want us to believe suppressing bad ideas leads to good ideas. It's a fundamental misunderstanding of human nature, which is at the root of every terrible progressive impulse. Humans are a communicative species. It is in our very DNA. We will find our tribes and our ideas will flourish there. When we drive discussion underground, we create dark corners, deep pockets of perverted thought. With no counter arguments, no illumination, the purveyors of these ideas begin to believe they are right. Their oppression further justifies their twisted thinking. Poor thinking grows like a mold when it cannot see light or fresh air. We create spaces for these ideas to expand when we force them into the dark corners. Big TechMedia and its leaders suffer from great hubris when it comes to this. They imagine every corner is theirs to bestow and adjudicate. They cannot and will not accept the ferocity and perseverance of the human spirit.

We have to fight for free expression and thought, not just because it benefits our ideology, but because it benefits every-one. It is a safeguard against destructive ideas. Terrible ideas should be shouted down and pushed to the fringes where they belong. Where we see racism, we must be allowed to shout it down. Where we see bigotry, we must be allowed to shout it down. Where we see injustice, we must be allowed to shout it down. If we are not allowed to shut down one bad idea, we'll soon be prohibited from shutting any bad idea down at all.

This is the path we are on, and we are hurtling towards the complete annihilation of discourse. Where discourse is shunned, bondage is welcomed.

Their solution to discourse is nefariously underhanded and should give us all pause. In fact, it should scare the hell out of you. How do we argue for rationale when the very definition of rationale is being changed on a daily basis?

It gets worse.

BigTechMedia is intent on shutting down competition altogether.

The post-election chaos which ensnared conservative pub-lications wasn't just about trying to shape our narratives. It was also about cornering the market on ideas and shutting conser-vatives not only out of discussion, but out of the marketplace.

Americans are the resilient sort. We will always beat a new path around obstacles. When conservatives were shut out of the news and commentary industry, Rush Limbaugh ignited a talk radio revolution. When conservatives were shut out of news television, Fox News came along to change the game. When conservatives seemed far behind the eight ball when it came to the internet era, Andrew Breitbart revolutionized online discourse and launched conservative thought into the atmosphere. Progressives may have a lock on Hollywood entertainment and mainstream news dissemination, but conservatives, forced to tread new ground, have managed to dominate talk radio and web news. Our resiliency has been the bane of progressive media's existence. They keep throwing up roadblocks and we keep working our way around them.

It's important to keep in mind while Big Tech has been cracking down on counter-culture accounts, they haven't purged us altogether—and they won't. For all the insane censorship on YouTube, you can still go there and find videos from conservatives about controversial issues. You can hear people disputing the transgender movement, you can even find pastors doing videos defending why they believe homosexuality is a sin. I'm a loud voice for conservative values on Twitter and while I've had my followers purged, I've never been suspended. At least not as I pen this book. There is still plenty of conservative fare on Big Tech platforms. There are two reasons for that. One is plausible deniability. The truth is, even the Big Tech overlords are aware there is a thing called the Constitution, and while they might not need to care much about it, they still risk legal complications if they completely ban entire groups of people from suing their platforms. It's best to simply squash the most influential and let those with a smaller reach fight for clicks amongst themselves.

The other reason is they need us. That might sound counterintuitive but it's true. Despite what the media would like you and me to believe, this country is pretty much split right down the middle, ideologically. It's sort of a cosmic balance, ebbing and flowing in one direction or another over time. It's like the mysterious balance between male and female births. If left

alone by nefarious forces like government edicts or bigoted
religious beliefs (like the idea that males are more valuable and
women are possessions, in some parts of the world), male-to-
female births maintain a remarkable balance. It's as if a Creator
has set the necessary mechanics of life in motion and provided
the perfect algorithm to keep the machine humming.

Twitter can do just fine without conservatives, but they
can't be the most lucrative in the social media space without
conservatives. It's simply a matter of numbers and profits.

There is an idea among environmentalists that Big Oil
doesn't care about human life; that they are out for profits, and
they don't care how many people die as a result. Big Oil, in fact,
has the secret goal of killing as many living beings as possible,
because Big Oil is populated by evil men. This idea doesn't
hold up to scrutiny. People use oil. It's not great business to
kill off your customers. They are happy to kill off the competition by lobbying against electric or other alternatives, but not
at the cost of eliminating the very people they need to purchase
their products. They can be greedy, or they can be serial killers,
but they really can't be both.

It's the same way with Big Tech. They are happy to work
to stamp out the competition, but it's not good business to kill
off your customers. Better to simply take out the influencers
who represent a competitive ideology and continue serving as
large a customer base as possible. This is a distinct advantage
conservatives have in the social media space, but we often forget our value. That should be a consideration in any strategy
we might have to try to tame the beast of Big Tech. Don't
forget they need us too.

That being said, it was a gross miscalculation on their part
to push the big players into a corner. The Jack Dorsey's of the
world have understandably been able to convince themselves
that no other innovators were coming after them. After all, they
basically invented the way we communicate now. It would go
to anyone's head. If you've taken a look at Dorsey recently, you
can see it has definitely fussed with his head in some way.

But I digress . . .

As the attempt to marginalize conservatives reached a fever pitch, many conservatives chose to simply exit the mainstream platforms. They went to alternative places like MeWe, a budding Facebook competitor, and Gab, a Twitter competitor. But a new Twitter-like platform had popped up in the preceding months. Parler suddenly exploded once mainstream social media began "the purge." Nearly overnight the fledgling platform ballooned to 20 million users, as conservatives began purposefully searching out alternatives to the Big Tech conglomerate. Conservative commentator Dan Bongino announced he was buying an "ownership share" of the platform and just like that, Parler became a viable alternative to Twitter and other microblogging sites.

One would think "the powers that be" in Big Tech would be happy to offload so many of the unwashed conservative masses, but it was the opposite. They wanted to have their cake and eat it too—make half of the country and their problematic politics disappear while maintaining the brand loyalty of average conservatives on their own platforms. As it turned out, they didn't want us to disappear from their user rolls, they just wanted us to disappear from public relevance.

Conservatives were finally becoming more vocal about their complaints and registered their displeasure with their feet. The usual smarmy subjects in the legacy media scoffed at the exodus. Many likened conservative displeasure with Big Tech to children picking up their toys and going home because someone else was being mean. They laughed, telling conservatives if they wanted to be free to say whatever they want, they should just build their own platforms. Stop whining, start innovating, seemed to be the sentiment.

Even many elite conservative pundits took this tact. Their argument was largely the same. If we're so upset with the status quo at Twitter or Facebook, then instead of whining we should just be building. It's still a free country, after all. The subtext was that somehow conservatives were not actual customers of Twitter just like everyone else and didn't have the right to express unhappiness with the product. I like to call that breed of pundit the Professional Contrarian. They have conservative values, but they live in liberal/coastal enclaves and travel in those bubbles. They're just as subject to the desire to be liked as the rest of us. They don't like to be associated with the unwashed masses of flyover country. They want to be Serious Conservatives™ who can go to a cocktail party on Capitol Hill and hear "Oh, you're one of the *good* Republicans. We like you" over and over again.

Professional Contrarians will take the opposite position of whatever you're taking, because despite what they say to get your clicks and your loyalty, they think you're just as stupid and ill-informed as their progressive counterparts do. It's a sad reality, but it's important to keep in mind that punditry is entertainment. If politics is Hollywood for the ugly, then punditry is academia for the insecure.

I, of course, am exempting myself from this judgment as a Californian pundit living in a coastal bubble. Obviously. It's my book and I can do that.

It all came off as so dismissive, particularly for the people who are supposed to be representing free thought. Yes, Twitter is a private platform that can do what they wish with their technology. But they've set themselves up as a "public square" and there are certain constitutional protections that supposedly come with that. You can't forcefully segregate people in the public square. You can barely do it in the private square.

Bake the cake and all that.

It's one thing to tell people to set up their own alternative communication platforms; it's quite another to tell them to do it when their ideological enemies basically own the internet.

In January of 2021, Google and Apple removed Parler from their app stores, claiming those were platforms used to plan the January kerfuffle at the Capitol. This was yet another chilling step toward Big Tech being the final arbiters of truth and justice. It isn't up to a social media platform to play FBI, but here we are. The real blow came when Amazon took Parler off their mainframe servers altogether.

The Professional Contrarians had no answer for what to do when you're literally banned from the internet. How do you build a whole new internet?

It was a tough lesson for all of us. The Professional Contrarians may have been annoyingly and unnecessarily obtuse, but they did touch on an issue we all failed to take seriously. The rise of internet culture was a boon for conservatives, and a great tool in the advancement of capitalism and individual entrepreneurship. Perhaps no other group took more advantage of the opportunity to circumvent the system of status quo than conservatives. The rise of conservative online media changed the landscape of news and opinion forever. It was an impressive takeover of the online space.

But while we were congratulating ourselves and laughing at our liberal counterparts as they complained about our expanding internet presence, we turned a blind eye to the vast amount of power we were giving to social media entities. We were all thrilled to discover we could marshal Twitter and Facebook and other later platforms to serve a huge audience. These days your Facebook presence as a business is every bit as valuable as your website. It was delightful to be able to use social media to support your own business. We didn't even notice as the water started to get warmer and warmer. We were the frogs simmering in the pot. By the time we realized places like Facebook and YouTube held significant power over our livelihoods, it was too late.

Conservative innovators and investors probably should have been working long ago on securing their own servers and platforms. It just seemed unthinkable that Big Tech could grow powerful enough to skirt the Constitution.

Necessity is the mother of invention, as they say. Conservative-centric sites like Parler, Locals, and Rumble have been forced to not only build their own platforms but build the technology to protect those platforms. I'm a proud member of Locals, a Patreon-type platform that gives creators and their fans a chance to interact directly. Creators don't need to depend on YouTube or Google ad shares to earn their money.

Now conservative creators can go directly to the source—their fans. And as a bonus Locals has worked to set up their own safety net. They won't be feeling the wrath of Amazon or other Big Tech overlords with fascistic intents. They've built independence out of the bondage of censorship.

That's really the American way, and we were slow in getting there but there's no doubt now conservatives have learned their lesson. This is an exciting time in internet culture.

A PRECARIOUS TIME

The legacy media is furious. In a December 2021 interview, CNN's Brian Stelter was nearly apoplectic at the realization that conservatives weren't just disappearing due to Big Tech crackdowns, they were simply making a new path for themselves.

> "I think big picture, Pamela, here's the concerning trend line here—people are going more and more into their own echo chambers, more and more into their own bubbles, especially Trump voters. There's this new social media app called Parler getting a lot of attention because conservatives are leaving, saying they're leaving Twitter and Facebook, going off to Parler because they believe Parler is a safer space for them," Stelter continued. "What we're seeing is even more of a bunker mentality in right-wing media, and ultimately that's not good for the country."[4]

It is a rather pathetic irony that a man like Stelter is worrying about conservative echo chambers even as Big Tech and Big Media combine forces to delete one half of America from public conversation. They build their bubbles daily, kick out people who don't belong, and then fret that those people are just finding some other place to hang out.

I guess we are all supposed to just hang it up and go home to enjoy what our Facebook algorithms choose to let us see and choose who is worthy of our time based on who is worthy of keeping an account on Twitter.

These are not serious people, but their mentality is dangerous, and we've spent far too much time patting ourselves on the back for beating the first iteration of Big Media in the Rush Limbaugh era, and not enough time preparing for the next.

What we witnessed in 2020 and the months ensuing was the perfect storm of culture. The nexus of Trump Derangement Syndrome, COVID panic, a contentious election, and a summer of violent protests (or peaceful, depending on how you view burning down entire neighborhoods) created the perfect conditions for a media takeover of culture.

And make no mistake, media took over the cultural direction with a vengeance. People were starving for news and information. COVID was an unknown quotient and information, and theories were coming from every direction. We looked to the news outlets more than ever to deliver the latest on what we should do and how we should proceed.

The liberal legacy networks (who rule the space in quantity, if nothing else), in turn, continued with their same doom-and-gloom reporting on everything from this novel virus to tax cuts. Maybe more than at any point in modern history, Americans were glued to their news channels. Everything they fed us was digested, and I don't know when the last time was you sat and watched a few hours of an outlet like CNN, but most of what they were and are feeding viewers is straight-up trash.

No wonder our national psyche was getting ill. The media suddenly had the nation's full attention and according to them, we'd never been more divided (we fought a civil war to the tune of 600,000 American lives, but whatever), we'd never been in more danger, and we'd never been more racist (slavery, anyone?). Every miserable observation they made about Trump and Republicans and COVID responses was taken as gospel by a huge number of Americans.

The Swine Flu pandemic of 2009 barely registered in the media. I was a new mother at the time and in fact I didn't even know the threat existed until it had already passed. That's because Obama was President, and media coverage was vastly different than for the current pandemic. To be fair, the current pandemic is much more of a global phenomenon. It wasn't just us who shut down, it was everyone.

Excuse me while I take a brief sidebar to muse about this. Perhaps this is to overstate the influence of Donald Trump, but I wonder if Trump had not been President during the initial outbreak if other world leaders would have reacted as they did. It sounds ridiculously conspiratorial, but I think the specter of Trump played a large part in how panicked some big world leaders got and that spread to the other places that didn't really care about Trump but were just following the leads of other players. Perhaps if Hillary Clinton had been president this virus would have been no worse in the eyes of the media than the swine flu.

A gross speculation, to be sure. Welcome to my brain, where my mind's journey takes many winding paths.

I digress again. The point I'm making is when all you eat is onions, everything around you starts to smell like onions and every breath you take reeks of onions. When you're steeped in gloom, it gets absorbed into every part of your body.

Americans were given no hope from their media. Only a creepy COVID death count chyron and day after day of now proven fake news on Trump's supposed Russian collusion, White supremacist attacks on B-list celebrities in the dead of a Chicago winter night, and complete panic regarding every member of Trump's administration, either coming or going. Poor Betsy DeVos was called everything but a child of God for suggesting parents should be able to choose where their kids go to school.

If you only watched legacy media, you couldn't help but be an absolute basket case. I can't blame people for succumbing to the hysteria. Coupled with Big Tech censorship and sprinkled with fake news, it all added up to a new Cold War of information. "We have never been so divided" became the mantra.

It wasn't how the average American was actually living. Most people in America live and work with people who are fundamentally different from them and get along just fine, but the narrative didn't reflect that. It was a drumbeat that had a direct effect on our national conversation. Network stars like Joy Reid and Brian Stelter fueled the fires of discontent by deliberately framing America as teeming with racism. They propped up hoaxes like the Jussie Smollett case. They salivated over every hate crime hoax, and there were plenty. They declared verdicts on controversial issues before evidence was even gathered, adding to the growing angst among average citizens.

Look at the Kyle Rittenhouse trial. As a quick recap for the few people who may have forgotten, Rittenhouse was a seventeen-year-old boy who ended up killing two men in self-defense after he took a rifle to help protect his neighborhood businesses during Black Lives Matter rioting in Wisconsin. From jump, the usual suspects in progressive media labeled this a hate crime. They immediately described the young man as a White supremacist. They insinuated he'd traveled many miles "across state lines" with the intent to murder Black protesters. Many progressive pundits and social media keyboard warriors reported Rittenhouse had murdered two Black men in cold, Klan blood. All this before a shred of evidence had been revealed.

Of course, everything they said about the case was wrong. Not just wrong. Completely, totally, absolutely, tragically wrong. It is perhaps the greatest act of media malfeasance I have seen in many years.

Rittenhouse didn't "travel across state lines" (as if any of those people knew what that was supposed to mean anyway). He technically crossed a state line, but it was mere miles from his mother's home (his home) on the Illinois border to his father's home (his home) on the Wisconsin border. People in border towns cross state lines every day. It was inconsequential but the legacy media kept repeating it as if it were meaningful, and thus so did their viewers.

Rittenhouse didn't hunt down anyone but was pursued until he turned his weapon on his pursuants in self-defense.

Most importantly, Rittenhouse didn't kill two Black protesters. No one in this story was Black. All three of his attackers were White, and none of them were of good repute. Two were convicted pedophiles. Yet the legacy media insisted, and to this day insists, on painting this as a racial hate crime. It was a narrative they committed to, and a lie they perpetrated for their own enjoyment.

The cognitive dissonance was astounding. Even after many of them wised up to the fact there were no Black victims involved in this story, legacy talking heads couldn't let go of the talking point. They pivoted to the idea although the victims weren't Black, they were standing up for Black people and thus, they were still victims of a hate crime. It was an astonishing pivot but done with such boldness it almost commanded a certain about of respect. It takes a lot of chutzpah to just lie, get caught in a lie, and then just paint the lie and sell it anyway.

Luckily for Rittenhouse, the entire encounter was caught on video, and it helped persuade a jury to acquit the young man. The video, of course, was simply memory-holed by the legacy media. They refuse to let go, because doing so would be to admit not only were they wrong, they were lying.

Following the verdict, online America erupted in accusations of White supremacy and systemic racism at work. Celebrities took to their accounts to issue breathless remarks about racism and the victory of White supremacy. Talk show hosts took Very Serious Moments in the middle of comedic monologues to reprimand America for our cruelty and racism. To be sure, not one of them had even the slightest clue about the video, evidence, or the trial. Yet every one of them was righteously outraged.

What do you call someone who lies to you constantly? What do you call someone who feeds your fear instead of your wisdom? What do you call someone who tells you to hate, and tells you that you are morally superior for your hate? What do you call someone who is always whispering in your ear to alienate the people you love if they think differently from you or vote differently from you? What do you call someone who actively roots for the demise of people they disagree with? What do you call someone whose only commodities are discouragement and rage?

Perhaps you feel the term "enemy" is harsh, but does that describe a friend?

I say this without irony or regret. Trump was right. The mainstream press is the enemy of the people. If you are to go by my description above as indicative of their characteristics, there is no other way to describe them. Another apt description from the late, great Rush Limbaugh is drive-by media. These people pull up to a playground, stick a gun out the car, and spray bullets everywhere, and then take off, leaving the innocent bystanders to clean up the blood and the wreckage while they just head to the next offense.

They toy with us for ratings. These are the people we put our trust in to inform us, and instead they do the exact opposite. Most of them know the things they are saying are ridiculous. They know they are leaving out vital information and, in some cases, just lying. They don't care. They laugh at us in our angst and our family in-fighting and our bickering. They point and laugh, and then they get in their expensive cars or limos and head back to their cozy coastal bubble condos and continue their lives as they always have. They feel no need to unite, no need to comfort, no need to advocate for peace or understanding. Nothing in their lives changes while we're all at each other's throats. It is the most perverted sort of elitism, made worse by the fact they genuinely believe themselves to be heroes who speak truth to power.

The media used to be us. Now they are just another version of the inside-the-beltway swamp creatures. No, they are worse. They are the disease-infected genitals of the swamp creatures. At least the swamp creatures pretend to represent their constituents and occasionally come through with results. The legacy media does nothing but make us all itchy and enflamed.

Their bias creates the very bubbles that insulate us from each other . . . on purpose.

Let's do a thought experiment. What would happen if tomorrow the legacy media started running wall-to-wall stories on how the Biden Administration had finally successfully defeated COVID and—wow, look at that—cured systemic racism to boot? Would the narrative be challenged outside of conservative circles, or would your COVID notifications finally stop being shoved down your throat?

I contend that the relationship between media, BigTech and the Democrat-run portion of the D.C. Swamp is so sin-sick and symbiotic it would take but a word from any one entity to end all of the hysteria. They have cultivated an incurious audience in the city-centers, which are dominating COVID policy discussions right now. When Fauci said it was stupid to want to wear a mask, they all nodded along and shamed people who were desperately searching for masks to wear. When he said cloth masks were unsanitary, they joined him in ridiculing people in cloth mask. When he said masks were the only way to save America, they went all-in on masks. There are too many people who see their politicians as gods and rulers, and many of them are devoted progressives, the people fussing the most.

BigTechMedia has an outsized reach in shaping the conversation around any topic, but they don't have an undefeatable reach. Sometimes it might seem like there's no way to win against this cabal, but I beg to differ. There are some strategies to employ, some you can do from right where you are and some that require men and women of a certain means. This BigTechMedia cabal is maybe the most dangerous combination of powers we've seen in history. They want to be the people to define context and that is chilling.

Who gets to decide what's news? Who gets to decide what information you're allowed to see? Who gets to decide what the good ideas are and what the bad ideas are? These are the pressing questions, not necessarily for them but surely for us. We have to make it pressing for them as well.

They have the power to redefine language, whitewash history, and censor competing information. We've already let them go too far, and it's fair to say most of us were complicit in that. But it's not too late. This battlefield might be the most important.

It's time for conservatives to get serious about this front.

WHAT CAN YOU DO?

Spend your money

If you have money and the means to invest, be an innovator. Successful conservative influencers like Dan Bongino and Dave Rubin used their financial and social clout to join up with investors and tech entrepreneurs to create free-speech platforms that offer direct competition to mainstream social media. Just a few years ago we were all at the mercy of Big Tech. If you found yourself de-platformed, your options for continuing to earn an income were severely limited. Now there are options, and the silver lining to the Parler debacle is right-wing tech companies began innovating new ways to break their independence from big players like Google and Amazon. It's still a work in progress, but if we can set aside fear for a moment, this can be an exciting time. Right-wing media surged because of the internet. It was the Wild West, where anyone could go to make their fortune or start something new if they just had a few of the right tools. The right-wing internet will be the same kind of place and it would not surprise me at all if the right-wing independent internet sees the same sort of success that right-wing media saw.

Obviously, most of us are never going to be millionaire tech investors, but we have a small part to play here if we so choose. Besides patronizing free-speech platforms, those of us who are skilled or interested in tech and programming should endeavor to go to work at places like Google and Facebook. Apply for those jobs at startups, work your way up to the Twitter Safety department. *Get a seat at the table* is what I'm saying. The reason these platforms can act so biasedly is because there is no one around them to tell them not to. They all think they're doing the right thing because everyone in the circle thinks like they do, talks like they do, and votes like they do. There's no moderation for the moderators. Become the moderators. Become the adjudicators. And if you're brave enough, become the dissenters. However, I'm not suggesting you become a professional thorn in the side of Big Tech. I'm suggesting you BECOME Big Tech.

I've heard rumors that a couple of the biggest conservative sites out there have deals with Facebook on the down-low. They basically pay for the privilege of not being censored. While that may seem distasteful to the "bootstraps" crowd, I begrudgingly favor it. They are playing the game. And just like we didn't see the abuses coming while we were handing over more and more of our lives to Big Tech, there's a good chance they won't see the power shift until it's too late for them. I am definitely in favor of playing by the rules they set up and using those rules to circumvent their insanity.

Speaking of which . . .

Make them play by their own rules

This goes for BigTechMedia in general. Just like with cancel culture, none of this changes until everyone is forced to play by the same rules. It's creepy how much alt-left progressives insist on using the term "misinformation" these days, but if they're going to be out there snitching on accounts for spreading real information they are too obtuse to know is true, then by all means we should be reporting accounts for the misinformation they spread. Take advantage of the rules defining "harmful" posts. Many times, conservative accounts get banned on places like Twitter or Instagram not because the moderators were seeking to ban conservative content, but because those accounts get spammed by complaints in coordinated efforts. At some point the algorithm just says they have to go.

It's not the most gracious thing but you don't have to make up things to report. Online progressives regularly report misinformation. I've reported tweets from the World Health Organization, celebrities who misquote the science on masks, or pundits who put words in the mouths of other personalities just for clicks. It's not a fun game, but it's one that two can play. If we can't change the rules, we might as well use the rules to do exactly what they do.

It would be nice to get back to a place where people can just say what they think and everyone else just goes on with their lives. That will never happen if the progressive left in media and Big Tech aren't forced to live on their own field of play. They'll go back to "people can say what they want" when what they want to say is treated with equal scrutiny.

Sue the hell out of the media

Nick Sandmann, the Covenant Catholic student who was slandered by the entire legacy media for a single picture that completely misrepresented his situation, should represent a roadmap. Sandmann was the victim, a child being bullied by a grown man, and instead was accused of being a White supremacist bully simply because he was wearing a red cap. He and his family sued CNN for libel and won and most recently sued MSNBC and won. Sandmann is set to be a very wealthy man for the rest of his life if and when the media companies pay up.

It was an egregious abuse of journalistic influence, and Sandmann went through a tortuous public indictment, for such a young man. But the silver lining was a new path emerged for conservatives to push back against the smears and lies we've become so used to fielding from the legacy press.

Sue 'til the wheels come off.

Kyle Rittenhouse has indicated he plans to do the same thing, given that the media not only accused him of being a White supremacist but also rendered a verdict for him before he even received his due process.

James O'Keefe of Project Veritas is currently embroiled defamation suits against the *New York Times* and Twitter. John Stossel is currently suing YouTube for demonetizing his videos over verifiable facts they claim are false. For years conservatives resisted legal action as a tool against overreach. We have a natural distaste for our litigious society. However, again, if we can't make the rules, then we have to exploit the rules.

Conservatives who can afford it should be suing the media for defamation or libel whenever a case is viable.

Bankrupt legacy media.

Support independent journalists and creators

Reporter Sharyl Attkisson was one of the premier reporters at CBS through the Obama administration. Her work had won her Emmys and she was highly regarded among her peers. That is, until she started looking deeper into some of the scandals of the Obama administration, including the terrorist attack in Benghazi. Attkisson contended that the higher-ups at CBS were preventing her from being too inquisitive about Obama's scandals. The honesty lost her a job at CBS and the support of her professional colleagues. Before Cancel Culture was a known quantity, Attkisson found herself one of its first victims.

She was pushed out of the mainstream and lost twenty years' worth of reputation and respect overnight. But Attkisson didn't fade away into obscurity. She was one of the first news personalities to marshal the internet to make her own, personal journalism outlet. She was her own news network. Attkisson's show, *Full Measure*, was a groundbreaker in online journalism. To this day I don't think she gets enough credit for how she revolutionized independent journalism, but what Attkisson did was ignite a new era of independence in information. Her efforts haven't gone unpunished. She continues to face harassment from government authorities, claiming in 2020 her computers and private files had been hacked by FBI. She continues to pursue a resolution.

What Attkisson did inspired a whole new generation of newsmakers. We take it for granted now that so many in the news business run their own shows and channels. Attkisson had some examples, but a lot of the path forward was unbroken ground. She's had her challenges but her innovation has proved to be successful. Losing a mainstream job is no longer a career death sentence.

This is the way conservatives get around the gatekeepers . . . independent creation. The internet has been a blessing in the respect it puts creators in direct contact with their audience. That means audiences can support the content they like and trust directly. That means we need to be willing to support the content we like and trust.

I have often been approached by frustrated listeners and readers, telling me they feel taken advantage of by being asked to pay for certain portions of my content. Every content creator will tell you they've faced the same frustrations from fans. There is still a large portion of America that remembers when all TV was free, and it sometimes seems as if creators are being greedy by asking to be paid for their content, but it isn't like that at all.

When you support an independent journalist or creator with your subscription fees or your donations, you are helping their voices thrive and be heard. Tracking down a story costs time and money, and when you're not funded by a big conglomerate, how do you fund your investigations? The only way is to depend on the generosity and curiosity of your audience. Your support also frees all of us from being beholden to the ad gods, which are responsible for a lot of self-censorship. Losing a big advertiser can be a huge hit for the bottom line of an average creator.

I used to host a podcast called *Smart Girl*, alongside creator Teri Christoph and our mutual friend April Gregory. We discussed politics and pop culture from a conservative woman's point of view, and our show aired on a popular conservative podcast network. Our show was going strong through the

#MeToo movement, and when a New York woman came forward to tell a story about how she'd been allegedly abused by comedian Aziz Ansari, we naturally discussed it. After reading the story, we posited unanimously that while Ansari sounded like an entitled, awkward creep, he certainly hadn't engaged in sexual harassment. She engaged in sexual acts with him not once, but twice during their date, and stayed until he finally put her in a cab and sent her home. The young woman was upset the encounters weren't mutually satisfying and he had treated her so coldly once he'd gotten what he wanted. There were no allegations of physical abuse, but she characterized his behavior as abusive. At any other time, the story might have been a big nothingburger, but in the heat of #MeToo, Ansari's poor behavior looked even worse. His career still hasn't recovered from the accusations.

So, there we were, having a (what we thought to be) harmless conversation about nerdy comedians with too much money and no social skills and women who think having sex with a man they just met is the key to earning respect. We scolded Ansari for being a womanizer, but we also didn't think the woman herself should get out from under responsibility. We all agreed she was being a bit overdramatic, particularly in the face of truly terrifying stories of rape and sexual coercion coming out of the Harvey Weinstein scandal.

We thought nothing of it, until a major sponsor pulled their ads and we received a reprimand from the podcast network heads. They didn't fire us, but they put a muzzle on us regarding #MeToo or anything else related to the subject until further notice. We were only allowed to venerate accusers or make no comment at all.

It's not that the network agreed with the complaints of the sponsor. That wasn't the issue. The issue was the sponsors bring in a lot of cash, and cash is king. Principles can become secondary to cash flow, even in the world of so-called conservative activism. It's a reality I don't find to be right or wrong . . . it just is.

So while we weren't banned or blocked from the internet, our speech was chilled. Now we were self-censoring so the network could keep making their ad monies. Again, that's just how it is, but you can see how sometimes even "principled" conservatives are forced to bow to the pressure of the dollar. We all gotta eat.

It surely is annoying to shell out money here and there just to be able to find good content, but as you can see, your support is vital to keeping independent creators free and keeping information true. The creator who can pay his own bills through selling directly to you is the creator who will continue to seek out ways to entertain you and provide the information you're looking for. It's been a long, long time since the legacy media considered you their customer. Independent creators look at you as partners in the truth.

Pick some people to support. Join a subscription community for your favorite creators or journalists like Attkisson. Even if you don't chime in or watch that much, just the support is an act of rebellion against an establishment growing more resentful every day that conservatives are finding their own paths. It may not seem like a big deal to you, but every single content creator I know is so grateful for your subscription support, even if you think it's too small to be noticed.

Take your business to people who actually care about your business. Think of it as another way to ultimately bankrupt Big Media . . . which is what we need to do and do as quickly as possible.

CHAPTER 6

REWRITING HISTORY

*R*ewriting history and Critical Race Theory are two sides of the same cluster. CRT demands we deconstruct what we know about ourselves and rebuild it in their image. During the Summer O' BLM, we were forced to sit by while Antifa co-opted Black Lives Matter and joined with some of their more destructive members to loot, wreck, and burn down businesses and neighborhoods in cities across the country. While we were being told to be out in public in a pandemic was tantamount to murder, law enforcement was being instructed by Democrat politicians to stand down and let it all burn.

It was infuriating to watch, but the fury didn't end when the flames died down. Human nature is prone to overcorrection and America didn't just correct course after a summer of unrest, we veered into oncoming traffic.

As a Black American and a parent, I definitely have my complaints about the way we teach American history. It's not that I think we have too much "patriotic" content, it's that I think we don't have enough. We don't have enough because we rarely include the full breadth of the American experience.

For my children, Black history is a month, not an American experience. In places like our home state of California, we barely even recognize Black History Month anymore. It has been pushed aside by Gay History Month, which is totally separate from Gay Pride Month. There are so many rich stories to tell alongside our Founding Fathers, and also there are tragedies of our own making to tell as well. I think our public education system and the rest of us in general could do more to weave the Black experience into the general American experience. Black history is American history.

My point is, we have work to do. You may find this crazy but I'm thankful for the conversation that has been spurred by the ridiculous actions of the Black Lives Matter crowd. I loathe the Marxist organization, but their rage was so intense and so irrational, it really did force people to counter it with rational compromises. At the very least, a lot of Americans, particularly conservatives, endeavored to really dig into where they went wrong. No one (no decent person, anyway) wants to be thought of as a racist. The accusation was thrown around carelessly, and many of the complaints were based in fake news, but it did spur on some people to be more mindful of the legitimate complaints coming from the Black community. I found myself having conversations with White conservatives they never would have been willing to have five years ago. I appreciate the growth I've seen around the race conversation, and I admit it's not perfect, but I don't expect perfection. The difference between a conservative like me and the average progressive is the progressive thinks perfection is just one more law or rule away, and I think perfection is a person, God come as Man and given to us to help us walk toward a day of ultimate perfection. It's very freeing when you can accept perfection is divine, and you have no way to get there on your own. It's no wonder progressives are always so cranky. They sense they'll never get to where they're going.

Perhaps it is that grossly unreasonable desire to force perfection on the world around them that progressives are so prone to grossly overcorrecting. Their solution to whatever failings we've shown in our view of American history was not to fix anything, but to destroy it all. A rash of emotional and impulsive edicts from blue city mayors and officials across the nation saw Black Lives Matter deciding for all of us that any-thing even remotely recalling a time of racism or oppression should be completely removed from our sight.

LITERALLY CANCELING HISTORY

In fact, the day I wrote this chapter, the Teddy Roosevelt statue was removed from the New York Museum.

It's a bizarre notion we can erase the pain of the past by erasing the past. It is equally bizarre one might find themselves traumatized by the mere presence of statues representing bad actors in our history. America's greatest sin was slavery. We fought a civil war over the issue. It was bloody and it was trau-matizing. Bad people did good things and good people did awful things. Their stories shouldn't be erased because a few activists think people walk by a statue of Robert E. Lee every day and weep. If a statue is keeping you from reaching your full potential, you have a lot more problems than the statue.

I know some conservatives feel sensitive about the issue because it feels like activists are trying to erase the history of White people in America, and maybe they're right. That's an overcorrection and one that is extremely dangerous. They say history doesn't repeat itself, but it often rhymes. Anyone who thinks we can erase the unpleasant parts of our past by tucking away its symbols is a fool to believe we'll just remember the lessons without the symbols or the stories. I can remember September 11, 2001, almost like it was yesterday. The fear is still palpable to me, and I see everything in the present through the lens of that past event. And yet, it has taken only a single generation for our children to be totally removed from the event or even its memory. In the same vein, it was barely a generation before people began pulling away emotionally from Pearl Harbor. To me, it feels like a historical footnote. The horror has not been passed down, and I'm not sure if my children could even tell you what it was. I make sure they watch a documentary on September 11 with me every year, to keep the terror and the lessons of that day as fresh as possible. Pearl Harbor doesn't hold the same place for most people my age. That's how it goes.

It is foolish to think it won't take but a generation to forget the lessons of the past if we keep trying to erase the symbols. We are already teetering into the abyss of the rhyme. Critical Race Theory has been delivered to us on the backs of Black Lives Matter and with it has come a whole host of bad ideas, one being segregation. After the victory of the civil rights era, we are now seeing examples popping up all over of classrooms and schools and office spaces segregating their students and workers by race. It's not uncommon to have BIPOC (Black and Indigenous People of Color, for those of you who aren't one of the cool kids) safe spaces on a college campus. That's a place where White people are excluded, and it's not only considered acceptable, it is encouraged. By adults.

In Atlanta, a Black mother was infuriated when she called her daughter's school to have her moved to a classroom with a teacher she felt would be more suited to her daughter. She was promptly informed her daughter could not possibly be moved to that classroom, because that classroom was for White students only, and her daughter was in the class for Black students only. This was a scheme concocted by the Black principle, in some misguided effort to group children into "safe spaces." I'm not sure if they called the Whites Only classroom a safe space, since that would imply they are unsafe with Black people, but no one said they actually thought about this.

Of *course* they did not think about this at all. We are too far removed from the pain of the civil rights movement and now we are deliberately erasing the symbols that are left to poke at our hearts and remind us of that past. Whether some geographical regions love those bad symbols or hate those bad symbols, they still play an important role in informing our present. The appalling truth of this present moment is we are sliding back into what we once deemed evil, in the name of progress. This is what happens when you let history become victim to emotion.

In his brilliant Substack editorial letter, writer James Cary discusses the warnings we see in some of our favorite dystopian novels. He points out the frightening but inevitable realization any rational person should make in the face of those who seek to rewrite history for "the greater good." Who decides what the facts are? Who decides what is of value for us to know and what should be kept from us? Who watches the watchers?

> These dystopian nightmares are not as far away as we might think. It's not quite an equivalent, but the sum total of "agreed" human knowledge is Wikipedia, which is being rewritten all the time. But who is doing the rewriting? Who are the editors? And who edits the editors?
>
> Winston Smith and Mark Studdock are concerned with controlling the narrative, past, present and future. But in writing their novels, Orwell and Lewis demonstrated an even more profound truth: fiction is truer than history.
>
> Good fiction simplifies ideas so we can examine them more closely. Eternal truths are seen more clearly. And so these stories have a greater emotional resonance, and a longer shelf life. Classic fiction, like *1984*, *Fahrenheit 451* and *Brave New World*, stands the test of time.
>
> This is why the old stories must be undermined, laughed at or, in the case of *Fahrenheit 451*, destroyed. If you are found in possession of a book in Ray Bradbury's world, the fire brigade will come to your house and burn it to the ground. This is a story that understands the power of fiction and how socially subversive it can be.[1]

If you deconstruct history, you deconstruct wisdom. It is obvious some people want that.

I don't think it's wise to pretend like we have nothing to change here. I do think it's wise, however, that it is rational and sober people who are the deliverers of that change. Change is here. We're not going to shoo it away by complaining about the unfairness of it all, even as they haul away statues and erase past presidents from our view.

Instead of complaining and fretting, I propose we instead advocate for leaving our symbols in place and building up alongside them. Why remove a Confederate statue? The Civil War was a big deal. What about leaving it, and next to it building a memorial to Black Civil War soldiers or prominent abolitionists or anything we can draw on from that time that represents good and right. Some people can rage all they want, but it doesn't change the fact our history intertwines good and bad, inspiration and discouragement, violence and peace. None of these factors exists without the other in our story. We are fools to try to separate them. We will only end up separating ourselves.

WHAT CAN YOU DO?

For one, we can all start thinking about my previous proposal. What if we focused on building alongside? That would truly be "progressive." Erasure is regressive. On purpose.

This all goes back to making sure you are in a position to be a part of the change. When it comes to state and municipal properties, these decisions are made by committees and councils. Get on the committee, run for council. Stop ceding this territory to people who are hell-bent on destroying it all.

I am not talking about exclusive resistance. I'm talking about taking the wind out of the sails of the opposition by beating them to the punch. Let us be the people who take the lead and demand a more robust version of history in our schools and our parks. Let us be the people who dare our ideological opponents to tell us why burning legacies is better than building them. Let us be the people who lead the charge for change. Start proposing new memorials and statues and plaques and whatever else, ones that reach back to some of our forgotten heroes and help highlight our diverse past and present. How disarming would it be if instead of being defensive about Confederate statues being removed, we were on the offense in demanding those statues be accompanied by the truth of their history and the figures who fought them.

If we are the sum of our parts, then what happens to the equation when parts are missing? The deliberate erasure and retelling of parts of our complicated history can only serve to create an imbalance, not a realignment. Insistence on preserving even the less desirable symbols isn't about denying the fulness of our story. It is quite the opposite. I believe there is some legitimacy to the claim we do not pursue a robust telling of the story of America. I also believe no one has to be on the losing end of this new push to appreciate that robustness.

Instead of complaining the other side isn't "doing it right," let's be the people who guide America into this new era of understanding.

CHAPTER 7

CRITICAL RACE THEORY (HERE GOES NOTHIN')

I used to run an after-school program back in Gary, Indiana. Part of my job was to assist students with homework, run study sessions, and help them access the internet for school projects. This was back before everyone had a smart phone in their pocket and most people in the inner city did not own a personal computer. Our center offered kids a place to go to access the internet and find help and mentorship.

It was a really tough job and one I didn't choose on my own. My father-in-law, a local pastor of thirty-five years at the time, had procured a grant from the city for the center and invited me to head it up. What he saw in me, I do not know. Other than, I suppose, my availability. My first child was three by that time and I'd given up acting (okay, fine . . . barista-ing) to become a housewife and mother. I certainly had no experience in management or even children outside of my own. What I did have was a passion for justice, a heart to help, and a mother-in-law who swooned over my son and was eager to help care for him after his days at preschool. My schedule could be flexible enough for me to still be home for my husband and son most of the time, and when I couldn't be, my in-laws would care for him. We all lived within two miles of each other and frankly, I was needing a distraction from the monotony of wifehood and motherhood. Those were both jobs I took on willingly and earnestly, but I'd be lying if I said being a wife and mother isn't the hardest and often most boring job in the world. I think my husband and his father sensed I wasn't the type of woman to find fulfillment exclusively in the home and I was struggling with that. I would never have given up my status as a homemaker. I was proud of it, even if I wasn't good at it. Frankly, I think it is a calling and one most women should take up at some point. I'm not saying I was too good for it; I'm saying I wasn't good enough for it, and I knew it. I needed another outlet to indulge my need to be good at something. I suppose this seemed like a good fit for all of us. Flexible hours, loving family to help care for my son. I could be home before and after school and still have dinner on the table for my husband when he got home.

Of course, the funny thing no one tells you about non-profit work is that because it is an area most people go into because for their hearts, non-profit workers tend to work much harder than they originally think. They work long hours and when things are tight, they are the first to forego their pay. There's nothing to be done about that. It comes with the territory and it's why the average length of leadership in the industry is only a few years. Burnout is inevitable, but also a sign of great passion. If your organization is healthy and thriving, a new leader will come along to replace the outgoing one and then so on and so forth. The circle of life in the nonprofit industry.

So, I took the job, not knowing anything about education except my own, not knowing anything about children except my own, not knowing anything about mentoring except for my own mentors.

I've never been afraid of a challenge. In fact, there is a warped part of me that feels like something is wrong if anything is too easy. Struggle feels natural to me. I figured I could wrestle this experience into something useful, whatever happened. At the time I was also a default liberal. Like most of the people

around me, most Black people, I just assumed good people
voted for Democrats and bad people voted for Republicans and
that was that. I felt strongly about saving the poor and
oppressed from the evils of racist capitalist pigs. Gary was a
rough place and my introduction into inner city life had been
swift and merciless. I went from living on the north side of
Chicago in what was then Boystown (it is what you think it
sounds like) with six roommates and a fledgling theater career
to the murder capital of the United States at the time. A town
of less than 100,000 people, riddled with gangs and poverty
and corruption and drugs—it was a stunning shift, and I was
allowed no lead time.

I waded into the job, hopelessly naive but self-righteously
assured I could help people, that I had some answers. Our
humble "Tech Center" was in a desolate strip mall on the west
side of town. When my husband was growing up, that strip
mall had been a hotbed of activity. Next door was the roller-
skating rink, now nothing more than a sad, dilapidated husk,
covered in vines and loneliness. Back then it was the place to
be. Much of Gary was. It had risen on the banks of Lake Michigan on a bed of steel and collapsed when the steel mills pulled
up stakes and left for friendlier shores. My husband's family
were the first Black family on their street, something I always
found so difficult to picture. My only experience of Gary had
been as an exclusively Black and tragically destitute city. White
flight took whatever money was left in the city after the mills
closed, and the rest is history.

The mall was L-shaped and just big enough to make a
midsized parking lot look appropriate. The parking lot itself,
now devoid of roller rink fanatics and Saturday night cruising,
was in terrible shape. It was full of potholes and cracks. Weeds
filled the long-forgotten cracks decorating the lot, which was
only a tenth full on any given day. There weren't that many
people in Gary, but even fewer places worth driving. Our
westside strip mall had a Walgreen's, a carwash that was always
changing hands and never earning money, a rickety Chinese
"bulletproof"—a take-out joint with bulletproof glass between

the customer and the kitchen—a wig shop, a Vietnamese-owned nail salon, a corporate-chain tax accountant, and oddly enough, a stand-alone cell phone store I'm sure used to be an old drive-up Fotomat or something like that. Because it was not attached to the strip mall (it stood thirty feet off the sidewalk in the middle of the parking lot), it was always getting robbed—most of the time in broad daylight. After a while it became a joke. *The cell phone shop got robbed? Again?*

Our storefront center lay at the far end of the strip mall, next to the building manager's office. That might seem like a great place for us to be, but it was not. We were a non-profit, paying rent on time and in full every week, helping local kids and filled with good, hardworking people. We didn't put up with nonsense or bad behavior. But in the inner city, those qualities aren't always rewarded, and our building managers seemed to resent us for it. Perhaps because they knew we were honest and reliable, they were always trying to shake us down for lease violations, or other perceived issues. The maintenance workers harassed the women who worked for me every day when they arrived and every day when they left. My employees were subject to catcalls and rude comments and when one of the girls refused to except an invitation for a date with one of the workers, he hurled insults at her as she left for home, calling her a lesbian (and other less-flattering terms for women who like other women). One day we'd finished our work, and since it was the last day before a holiday break, I bought the children chalk, and we went outside to decorate the sidewalk in front of our store. As we closed, the manager walked over to tell us she'd be giving us a fine unless we washed the happily drawn pictures off the sidewalk. She called it a "blight"—even as the dilapidated cell phone store behind us was probably being robbed for the thirtieth time.

That is what we were up against and frankly, it is the attitude we are all up against these days. It is an attitude of entitlement, and really, resentment. It is resentment for those of us who choose to work to fix problems instead of simply wallowing in problems. Miserable people want miserable company.

It was in that atmosphere I realized I was miserable and silently asking people to share in my misery—as a type of penance for some, and a type of commiseration for others. I never would have thought of myself as a victim, but I sure didn't have a problem labeling others around me victims. Not until I came face-to-face with what that does to the psyche of a community.

Although I was still a liberal, I had already begun the first steps of my ideological shift. My beloved father-in-law was the first Black man I'd ever met who openly called himself a conservative, and we often had intellectual conversations about politics and culture. We disagreed often, but he never belittled me. Instead, he challenged my assumptions, and challenged me to expand my sources of information. He was a middle-aged Black man who had grown up in the last vestiges of Jim Crow and yet there wasn't a shred of victimhood to him. My own experiences with racism made me want to blame White America for everything wrong in our community, but Dad's life was a study in grace, and how far it can take you. Our conversations (and a chance encounter with the *Rush Limbaugh Show* one day) put me on the path to at least reconsidering some of my long-held assumptions.

There was a day when a lightbulb moment came for me, and it changed everything.

I was conducting a study group with my fifth graders, and we were talking about the upcoming holidays and the schedule for the Tech Center hours. I told the children my husband and I would be absent for much of the holiday as we were planning on taking a long-awaited "mom and dad, only" vacation to Jamaica. I was very excited about it.

Sidebar: Take your mothers-in-law's advice from time to time. She told me to book ten days for the vacation because I would get to day 7 and wish I had just a couple more. I told her I couldn't imagine leaving my son for that long and I would feel bad about burdening her. She just rolled her eyes and dropped her chin and gave me the old, "Mmmkay. Well, I tried to tell you." And she was right. Day 7 of the trip came and I said to myself, "I wish I had two more days!" So let that be a lesson to you. Sometimes your mother-in-law is right! In my case, it's most of the time.

It is important to note in this story and nearly every story from my time in Gary, everyone around me is Black. It will be relevant to my point. I could count the number of White people I knew in that city on one half of one hand. I remember their names to this day—that's how rare of a sight it was.

So here I am, sitting at this table with all these children I've come to adore, and I tell them I'm heading to Jamaica very soon. One of the girls looked up from the paper she was scribbling on and furled her brow. Her lips formed into a disapproving curl, and she looked straight at me.

"Jamaica??" she blurted, clearly annoyed and confused. "Why would you go to Jamaica on your vacation?"

I was genuinely perplexed. I mean, why *wouldn't* I go to Jamaica for my vacation? It's beautiful, tropical, and surrounded by pristine, blue ocean. I love the beach, I love to relax on the beach, and I love to drink on the beach. Jamacia sounded like the perfect place to do all of those things. Besides, my husband and I had both been burning the candle at both ends, professionally, personally, and in regard to our commitments to the community. We had just gotten his first "grown-up" bonus from work, and we thought we'd treat ourselves to our first "grown-up vacation" with it. What was so crazy about two people vacationing in Jamaica . . . particularly two *Black* people?

I asked her as much.

"What does that mean? What's wrong with Jamaica?" I responded.

"Nothing. It's just that . . . well . . . don't a lot of White people take vacations in Jamaica?"

I was speechless. I cannot describe the weight of the realization that hit me in that moment. I used the term "lightbulb" earlier but that doesn't quite get it. It was more like . . . a dawning. It was like when you witness a color change on a film screen, and you see the line begin at the top of the frame. As it slowly descends, it takes the previous color with it. Below the line is black and white. Above the line, as it descends, is full color. It makes its way to the bottom of the frame and leaves its subject with a whole new color scheme.

It was like that. A revelation washed over me.

I asked her, "Why would you say that?"

"I'm just sayin' . . . why would you want to vacation with White people? I wouldn't want to be around all those White people."

It was shock to the system. A cold splash of ice water on a blazing hot day. Two things struck me:

First, this little girl didn't know any White people. In fact, most of the children had limited contact with White people. We like to imagine "diversity" is something only those redneck communities in flyover country need to know about. But the truth is the inner cities of smaller urban centers can be every bit as isolated. It was the first time I'd ever really thought about how social/racial segregation is not always about Jim Crow. Sometimes it's simple isolation. Most people aren't deliberate about seeking out diversity. Black people are no different than anyone else.

The other thing that struck me was I realized I'd been spending so much time telling these kids the world was against them, and White America had no intention of letting them in the door, while at the same time I was telling them if they worked hard they could be whatever they wanted to be, they could propel themselves out of their circumstances. What I was really doing was encouraging limits on their vision for their own lives.

Why shouldn't they want to be able to afford a beautiful vacation to Jamacia one day? Why should they go through life imagining there were White spaces and privileges and Black spaces and privileges and never the two shall mix? It wasn't how I lived my life. How dare I encourage them to live that way.

And yet, that's exactly what the tentacles of Critical Race Theory (CRT) do to us. They separate us and pull us apart. They tell us we can only be happy and safe if we don't have to experience the lives of those who are different from us and who might feel superior to us.

My time at the tutoring center was transformational. I saw how the policies I supported as a liberal worked and it turns out . . . they don't. My heart turned toward my community in a way I wasn't prepared for. I began a journey that led me down a path to taking ownership of my life, my family and my community.

CRT isn't about ownership; it is about blame. It is about tearing down and rebuilding. It is about segregation in the name of justice. It is everything that just ten years ago we would have arrested someone for teaching in a classroom.

But let's not get too far ahead of ourselves. As I write there is a fierce battle taking place in school districts across the country. It has become messy. Very messy. It has spilled out from behind the closed doors of school board meetings and into the homes of every American as we watch video of angry parents and protests and hear story after story of school board recall after school board recall.

Critics accuse concerned parents of being racists who don't know what CRT really is and who only wish to prevent America's real racist history from being taught. The FBI has accused concerned parents of being possible domestic terrorists. There is a lot of accusation floating around, but not much progress. We'll see this is deliberate—but first . . . what is Critical Race Theory?

WHAT IS CRITICAL RACE THEORY?

You can't talk about Critical Race Theory (CRT) without understanding Critical Legal Studies, which is the parent of CRT. It is an academic pursuit, and as such is hard to define without giving you paragraphs and paragraphs of legalese that will neither interest you nor captivate you. I'm not a legal scholar, and you're not reading me to become one.

However, the fact I'm *not* a legal scholar and likely you are not either is very important to this discussion. Part of the reason the discussions have become so messy is that we are arguing over a type of theory that was only ever meant as a collegiate academic exercise. Academia is well known for its convoluted studies and analysis. The average American wouldn't typically be breaking down these extremely analytical legal theories on a daily basis but now we are being asked to do just that, but without the academic knowledge of the subject to stay on task.

In a nutshell—a very big, convoluted nutshell—Critical Legal Studies (CLS) is an analytical method applied to the justice system; analyzes the effects of politics on the legal system and posits the structure of our legal system cannot be separated from our social structure. The legal system is not an objective platform, but rather one that is influenced by political and social power structures and thus can implement justice disproportionately. CLS studies the influence of politics and society on the legal structure and proposes options for untangling them.

Now—and here's where the rabbit hole gets deeper—CLS itself is just a bastardization of Critical Theory, originated at the Frankfurt School. Critical Theory was a philosophy developed by German thinkers in the early twentieth century. By the school's own definition, Critical Theory critiques modernity and capitalism through the lens of a Marxist worldview.

I'm giving you this admittedly incomplete but quick rundown of definitions because I want to make sure you don't let anyone tell you that calling CRT Marxism is some kind of conspiratorial, fringe nonsense. It's right there in the history, and the originators use the term themselves.

Critical Race Theory is based on Critical Legal Studies and Critical Legal Studies is based on Critical Theory and Critical Theory is based on Marxism. Therefore, Critical Race Theory is Marxism—it is simply Marxism dressed in civil rights drag. That's the delineation.

Marxism is a completely impractical and an absolute failure of human ingenuity in every way possible for everyone who has tried, always. Marx spent a life being cared for by other people. His father, a lawyer, educated him at home until Marx was old enough to send off to law school. Marx then married a wealthy baroness which left him able to focus on writing and philosophy. The worst ideas in human history stem from idle men who have nothing to do but think and imagine and pretend they know the way of the world for those who choose not to or cannot be idle.

Marx had an idea of how the world should be, but it was not based in his experience of it. Instead, his ideas were based in how he imagined others experienced the world. Like many socialists, Marx probably came to his philosophy with the best of intentions. He had a loathing for the world of wealth in which he resided, and perhaps a compassion for the working class he crossed paths with every day. He saw inequity, but because he was a man who had been provided for his whole life, the solution to inequity seemed rather simple. The wealthy had more than the proletariat, so all that needed to happen was for the wealthy to give more to the proletariat. If the wealthy couldn't own their homes or businesses or luxuries, the working class would have access to more resources. To keep anyone from becoming wealthy, and therefore an enemy of the proletariat, a benevolent state should be the only owner and thus the only giver. A state run by the wealthy elite couldn't be trusted, but because in Marx's limited worldview there is automatic nobility in poverty, a state run by the working class would be the ideal government. If the state can control the means of production and distribution, the state can train its citizens to be equitable and live equitably. And of course, those running "the state" will always be equitable and well-intentioned and will never succumb to intoxicating power that comes with control of an entire society.

It is a childish way to view the world, and again, one aided in part by being a member of a class that has been provided much but earned little.

Marxism birthed Critical Theory, and Critical Theory seeks to upend "the system" from the inside out and build a completely new system, one in direct opposition to capitalism, which is a system that works on merit. Most children hate merit-based exercises. Earning things is something we have to teach our children. Every child will make do with just being given everything they want if we parents allow it.

I used to become so frustrated with my children when they were young and learning. In exchange for their modest allowances or an item they really desired, they had certain responsibilities around the house. Walking the dog, doing the dishes, performing the chores I'm far too old and far too good for anymore.

I would get so annoyed when I would ask them to do something and would be greeted with sighs or eye rolls, or both. Why can't these kids just do what I ask without the attitude? I'm not asking them to solve world hunger, I just want the trash emptied.

Soon enough I realized it didn't matter if they had attitudes about doing their chores—the point is they did their chores. Of course they don't like doing chores. Chores are work and no one likes to work at jobs they have no interest in doing. If my kids wanted the comfort of money in their pocket or a very special video game they just had to have, they had to know how to earn those comforts. They most certainly would have been happy to just take my money or take my gifts. Can you imagine any child putting up an argument for otherwise? Instead, I seized the opportunity to teach them about the value of earning something on merit rather than for simply existing. They never learned to be cheerful about their chores, and to this day I have never heard one of them say they were grateful for all the dishes they had to wash.

What also didn't happen is this: *I didn't end up with entitled children*. They have learned the value of work and what it means for their lives. They have learned merit, and merit is what shapes a healthy adult.

We currently have a lot of unhealthy adults who have achieved a lot of milestones in their lives but with very little merit. Marxism is the ideology of a man who didn't understand merit, because he was raised (and then married into) in a segment of society in which people just seemed to have things. And the things they didn't have, they got at some point.

That's why CRT seems like such a childish "fix" to such ancient and nuanced problems as discrimination and racism.

It eschews merit for entitlement, and when you endeavor to run a government or a hallowed institution like public school based on the principle of entitlement, you must necessarily engage in what's fair instead of what's right. Fairness is what gets you the gross and frightening immaturity in the classroom so many parents have been complaining about.

We've broken down the mechanics of Critical Legal Studies. It's actually not a completely crazy academic pursuit. After all, there is hardly a human among us who would disagree the legal system in America not always worked fairly for every citizen.

Just to say the name of Emmett Till should evoke an image of injustice for most Americans who know the name.

The Tulsa Race Massacre of 1921 saw thirty-five blocks of one of the wealthiest Black neighborhoods in America burned to the ground, with dozens (or hundreds by some estimates) left dead and thousands injured and/or displaced—all because a White teenage girl accused a Black teenage boy of assaulting her in an elevator. That boy was Dick Rowland, and his arrest ignited the flames of racism and hatred which ended up killing untold generations of Black wealth.

Medgar Evers was one of the most prolific civil rights activists of the era and he was gunned down in his own driveway by a member of the Ku Klux Klan. It took over three decades to bring his murderer to justice.

This list goes on and on. Our legal system is flawed and has not brought justice to all who have availed themselves of it, and particularly not for Black citizens over our most tumultuous years.

It seems like a logical intellectual pursuit if you're studying the law. One should want to understand the possible flaws in our system in order to represent the system properly. Critical Legal Studies is an analytical tool used to dissect the complicated and evolving world of the U.S. justice system, and to try to bring change to that system. Progressive talking heads are telling the truth when they say Critical Legal Studies is an academic pursuit that isn't being taught in K-12 curriculum.

That's as far as the truth goes with them on the issue. Because, as I've just laid out, CLS isn't the issue. CLS isn't what parents are getting riled up about at school board meetings. CLS isn't what is at the center of this debate. CLS is the nerdy child of Critical Theory, and CRT is its bastard offspring.

That's as far as I will go with my explanation of the mechanics of CRT. This isn't an informational book, it's an inspirational book. There are far better sources than myself if you wish to understand the nitty gritty of the issue, on both sides of the fence. In fact, I recommend you pick up Ibram X. Kendi's book on anti-racism and Robin DiAngelo's *White Fragility* if you're interested in exploring the details further. Maybe just check them out from the library if you don't wish to pay them for their prejudice. Those two tomes alone will help you understand the chaos and confusion that accompanies CRT.

I had the most trouble with this chapter, because there is so much information to explore and people have so many questions about what exactly the issue entails, and how to recognize it when it pops up. There were so many directions to go in, but this is not a book about CRT. This is a book about standing up for your rights and your principles and demanding to be heard.

It is, in fact, this very issue that made me decide I'd had enough. We were no longer talking about ideological differences. To me, this issue encompasses a battle between good ideas, and evil ideas. I cannot allow my children, or whatever children they might have, to inherit the perverted legacy Critical Race Theory seeks to leave them, under the guise of racial justice—a legacy of adopting wrongs to make rights, segregation, shame, hard-heartedness, and unforgiveness. It isn't just the idea of creating more racial animosity that worries me, it's the idea that every American experiment that has sought to upend our foundations—as turbulent and trying as they've been—has ended up striking the Black community first and worst. We will always be on the losing end of social experiments, even if we think—like the Kendi's of the country—that these are our ideas for our benefit. And anyway, this isn't even our idea. It is a White man's idea, repackaged and sold as justice to the Black community, that naturally will end up tearing us apart at the seams.

CRT evangelists in the mainstream media have made so many pivots on this issue it's enough to give one whiplash. As parents across the country began sounding the alarm about CRT incursions into the classroom, the mantra in the mainstream was, "CRT is not being taught in K-12 schools. It is a purely legal philosophy taught only at the collegiate level." As parents began to get more and more coverage of their outrage, the narrative shifted to, "Parents don't like CRT because it forces them to face their own racism." And finally we have ended up at, so far, "Parents object to CRT because they don't want their children to know history of racism, slavery, and oppression. They object to Black history."

Don't let any CRT televangelist tell you that you don't know what CRT is and what it means. If anyone ever tells you that, ask them to explain it. They don't know either, and the confusion and the malleable media narrative is proof.

COMMON QUESTIONS ABOUT CRITICAL RACE THEORY

Is Critical Race Theory just a misnomer for Critical Legal Studies?

No. Critical Legal Studies still exists and is still taught in academia. As I pointed out, Critical Race Theory is simply the bastard of Critical Legal Studies. Of course, it is real. A simple search of the internet will take you to numerous articles extolling the virtues of the philosophy. It is different than CLS precisely because it is an evolution of CLS. That is how all philosophy works. It begins in the halls of academia and if it is compelling enough it will eventually trickle down to the halls of your homes.

Everyone knows what communism is now, so much so that we take it for granted everyone knows what it is. However, at one time it was simply a concept discussed by philosophers and thinkers in the private salons of upper-class academia.

Are schools forcing CRT curriculum into classrooms underneath the noses of ignorant parents?

No. This is why the battles over this topic are so contentious. CRT does not come to our children in a lesson plan. It comes to their teachers in form of "equity training" and "anti-racist" seminars their unions and school districts provide during school breaks. It comes in the form of "discussions" in the classroom. It comes as an idea, not a piece of paper. The end result is to tear down some to lift up others . . . supposedly. The end result is always segregation.

Take the case of Atlanta mother Kila Posey. Posey called the principal of Mary Lin Elementary School, where her daughter attended, to inquire about placing her child in a new classroom. Apparently, she was concerned her daughter's current teacher wasn't meeting her needs and her daughter might do better with another teacher who would be a better fit. Posey was shocked to hear the principal say she could not relocate the student because that was not "one of the Black classes."

> "She said that's not one of the Black classes, and I immediately said, 'What does that mean?' I was confused. I asked for more clarification. I was like, 'We have those in the school?' And she proceeded to say, 'Yes. I have decided that I'm going to place all of the Black students in two classes.' "[1]

You can imagine this woman's shock. It is illegal to segregate schoolchildren, or anyone in any public institution, by race, among other qualities. It is literally enshrined in our federal Constitution and to my knowledge, every state constitution. Our grandparents and great-grandparents spilled blood, sweat, and tears to restore dignity to Black America, and now here was a Black, supposedly educated woman purposefully segregating her students by race. Not only that, explaining said segregation to a concerned mother as though it were the most normal thing in the world.

Posey has since gone on to file a discrimination complaint with the U.S. Department of Education's Office of Civil Rights. The Atlanta Public Schools district claims they have resolved the situation and do not condone the actions of the Mary Lin Elementary principal, but they have not been specific as to what their resolutions involved.

It would be helpful if Critical Race Theory were just a neon sign attached to every lesson plan and conversation in our schools and workplaces. It doesn't work like that. CRT comes couched in language like "anti-racism" and "equity" and what kind of a monster could be against fighting racism or promoting equity?

Those are just buzzwords. Their applications are far more nefarious. Anti-racism is the language of coercion. According to the gospel of anti-racism, it isn't simply enough to declare oneself "not racist." One must actively be framing everything through the lens of race and thus actively be opposing racism. If you are not actively exposing and opposing racism in every area, you are actively supporting racism. We can see the ridiculous outcropping of this philosophy in even the most neutral aspects of human endeavors, like math.

Recently, there has been a push to dismantle "White supremacy" in the field of math education by instituting "anti-racist" math instruction. At a website titled Equitablemath.org, educators can find a curriculum toolkit to help them combat White Supremacy in math. Their home page describes their program as thus:

> *A Pathway to Equitable Math Instruction* is an integrated approach to mathematics that centers Black, Latinx, and Multilingual students in grades 6-8, addresses barriers to math equity, and aligns instruction to grade-level priority standards. The Pathway offers guidance and resources for educators

to use now as they plan their curriculum, while also offering opportunities for ongoing self-reflection as they seek to develop an anti-racist math practice. The toolkit "strides" serve as multiple on-ramps for educators as they navigate the individual and collective journey from equity to anti-racism.[2]

I could spend this entire book breaking down the insanity that is passing for racial justice in this toolkit but that's not my purpose here. Perhaps the best representation of what this "math instruction" toolkit proposes to accomplish lies in their list of definitive concepts of "White supremacy" in the table of contents. Keep in mind, these are extremely common definitions in the anti-racism ideology.

> • *Perfectionism* • *Sense of Urgency* • *Defensiveness* •
> *Quantity Over Quality* • *Worship of the Written Word*
> • *Paternalism* • *Either/Or Thinking* • *Power Hoarding*
> • *Fear of Open Conflict* • *Individualism* • *Only One*
> *Right Way* • *Progress Is Bigger, More* • *Objectivity* •
> *Right to Comfort*[3]

What on earth any of these ridiculous things has to do with math should be beyond any logical person. If asking students to get the right answers to a problem and be on time for class is White supremacy, then every single math teacher and every single math problem in the history of mankind is White supremacist.

Which is kind of the point and very much the problem.

The Church of CRT makes White supremacy the devil. Just like the "satanic panic" of the 1980s, it demands we see Satan around every corner, in every interaction, in all our activities. Where the mantra used to be "the devil made me do it," now it is "White supremacy made *you* do it."

Unfortunately, there is no salvation, no savior to pay for our sins and rescue us from the satan permeating our every interaction. There is only blame. Under this new system of anti-racism, imagine what it would take for us to declare victory over racism. Just ponder it for a moment. What exactly would it take? Who is to decide what a truly equitable and non-racist society looks like? Do we really think the people who work themselves into power positions on the back of anti-racism would ever at any point declare the problem solved?

Whenever you hear anyone make the disingenuous claim that CRT is not in our schools, remind them CRT is in our teacher trainings and they are being told the only way to prove they aren't racist is to convince their White students they have inherited White supremacy, and that is in their DNA.

Think about the students in that Atlanta district, both White and Black. Think about the subconscious and irreparable damage segregation is doing to their psyches. They are literally being taught to view each other as "other," to view each other suspiciously. They are being taught they don't deserve to be together and be educated together. How can anyone possibly think segregating children leads to any kind of equity *or* equality? How can you view another person as equal to you in dignity and purpose when the authorities in your life tell you you're not even allowed to sit together in the same classroom?

Think about the teachers who quietly supported that system of segregation. Think of how many had to tacitly agree, and how many others were simply too afraid to speak up about the absurdity. Think about all those students could have learned from each other, and now they are denied the privilege of sharing their lived experiences in the classroom because of this perverted philosophy.

Nothing about this is okay. We cannot let it be okay. It will never be okay, and as a Black mother it breaks my heart. I would never approve of someone telling my children they are inferior because they are Black and they have inherited some kind of cultural sin. I cannot approve a White mother's child being told the same thing. Even if I were that kind of cruel, logic tells me segregation never benefits the Black community. We are only 13 percent of the current population of America. We will always be on the losing end of segregation, and that is proven at every juncture in history in which it has been tried.

Do people hate critical race theory because they hate Black history?

Look deep into my eyes (pretend you can see them in the words on this page and imagine they are the most beautiful eyes you've ever seen). Breathe in deeply and inhale this important, unassailable truth. Listen closely, and let the words be etched on your (likely racist) heart:

Critical Race Theory is not Black history.

This is how we know the left is not serious in their criticisms of right-wing America's opposition to CRT. At first, they tried to tell us CRT didn't really exist outside of higher education. Then they tried to tell us there is no such thing as CRT in K-12 schools, and now they tell us there *is* a push to get CRT in schools, but CRT is merely Black history and conservatives won't allow it because they hate Black history.

I don't need to rehash this. You, dear reader, are intelligent enough to recall what was written mere paragraphs ago in this chapter. We have established what CRT is and while I believe there are terrible people in every sector of life, anecdotally I must say I have never in my life personally met anyone who has said they would like to ban Black history from the classroom. Good heavens, we have a whole month dedicated to Black history. I, for one, would prefer Black history to simply live under the umbrella of American history, but that is neither here nor there at this point. It is patently ridiculous to suppose there are millions of Americans out there actively working to expel Black history from American classrooms.

But that's what all this is—ridiculous. From start to finish. If you wonder why it feels like every single thing in our lives has become politicized, it's because every single thing in our lives has become politicized. Even our children have been politicized. That is because the progressive left's faith system is politics.

ETERNAL HELL

As a Christian, everything I do and think and say is steeped in a worldview based on my faith. There is nothing about who I am that isn't impacted in some way by the gospel of Jesus Christ, and I think almost every person of every faith would say pretty much the same thing about themselves. Faith is intrinsic.

That is why, for the modern progressive, all of this is not rooted in opinion and disagreement, but rather in the very battle between good and evil. It is a faith system, and their worldview is intimately connected to that faith system. This is why you can't have fun (if occasionally contentious) arguments with your progressive friends and relatives anymore. This is why you used to be able to end a disagreement with a joke or roll of the eye and move on with your lives together, but no longer. What used to be political belief is now deep-seated faith on the progressive left. It really is about the battle for your soul, and your worthiness as a human being.

Critical Race Theory is a degrading philosophy, a bum religion, and it can't solve the problems of human nature. Power is power, no matter whose arms embrace it. It says everything we do and think is steeped in White supremacy, and the only way to defeat it is to completely dismantle the system and rebuild it. In the classroom it manifests itself as a type of discrimination, like we saw in the Atlanta case. It requires White Americans to be both apologetic and silent, vocal about anti-racism and quiet about everything else, loud about their own sins but mute about the sins of others. It simply seeks to exchange one evil for another, and I, for one, cannot abide by that. The pandemic brought us the cliché "we're all in this together," but somehow that stops short of solving racism. We all have work to do, but CRT tells us only White people have work to do, and they need to do it by disappearing from all conversation and solutions.

I hate to break it to everyone, but White people are still a huge portion of this country. We're not going to solve racism without them.

If we think of progressive politics as a faith, then we can think of CRT as a fundamentalist denomination—a cult, even—that seeks to control sin by controlling man. It began with some good ideas in the CLS sector. There are a lot of good ideas out there that become co-opted by man's need to control his environment and the people around him. This one is no different. We are being asked to swallow a Kool-Aid that will eventually strike us all down, regardless of race. In some cases, we are being forced to swallow it.

Do I sound too harsh? Think about the religious fervor surrounding this issue. Like religious institutions of old, ones that were perversely connected to government and rule of law, the Church of CRT demands we all worship the same god or be excommunicated.

If historical religion is man's attempt to find relationship to God, CRT is modern religion without relationship. It is the gospel of envy dressed up as justice. It has all the principles of a religion without the apparatus of a Creator who can dispense divine justice with loving grace. It is judgment without redemption. It is punishment without rehabilitation. It is forgiveness without grace. It is works without faith. It is separation without reconciliation. It is condemnation without restoration. It has all the hallmarks of a religion without the mechanics that make religion a viable human pursuit.

It leaves no room for grace or evolution of the spirit. It is eternal hell.

In the end, we can have endless arguments over the academic merits of CRT. We can pretend it has anything to do with Black history; we can pretend it's about racism or justice or equity. We in fact are being asked to pretend it is about that.

It is about none of those things. When we look at its purpose and we look at its application in school lessons and equity training, we can see it is not a system designed to right wrongs, but to repay wrong with more wrong. It is a belief system, not an academic tool. It is religion.

And now we're selling it to our children.

SPACE FOR GRACE

Some may read this and think, "Kira has lived a sheltered life. She's never had to face the reality of racism." Some may think I've sold my soul to the White man. As a conservative woman who is Black, I've certainly heard that many times before. If I were a weak-minded woman I might find it insulting. But I am old enough to know that those who hate you will fill in the blanks of your life with whatever they please, to make whatever point they wish about you. I remain unbothered. I've yet to meet a single adversary who knew a damn thing about my life—who I love, who loves me, where I've been, where I'm going, who I've helped, and who has saved me over the years, from life and from myself. They know nothing, so I refuse to feel angst over terrible guesses about my personal life based on what they think my voting pattern is.

My opposition to the twisted gospel of CRT has nothing to do with my own ignorance. It is my personal experiences with racism, both as a child growing up in Eastern Canada and as an adult American citizen that give me clarity. I know racism is sin, and the remedy for sin is forgiveness—not more sin, not more cruelty, not turning the tables in some kind of reckoning.

When my family and I first moved to America, we moved next door to a White family who had a little girl about the same age as my son. They were both in elementary school and became fast friends and could be found playing together nearly every day. It was a relief to us our son had at least found one friend to help ease his transition into a new life, away from everyone he'd known and loved. We smiled every time he announced he was heading out to play with this little girl I'll call Carrie, for the sake of anonymity.

One day, our son came running into the house, weeping angrily. We were shocked. He was never the type of kid to be very expressive. Something was obviously seriously wrong. We sat him down and begged him to tell us. Through unrelenting tears, he told us Carrie's dad had just come out to tell the children they would no longer be allowed to play together. He did not wish Carrie to continue being friends with our son.

"He said we are too different, and people like them can't be friends with people like us." He continued, heaving into my shoulder.

My husband and I looked at each other over his head. I think my heart stopped; my husband scoffed and rolled his eyes, shaking his head as he looked down at the floor in amused disbelief. We both knew what this meant. Neither of us is unfamiliar with either open racism or hidden racism. It just came as a bit of a shock. You always imagine California to be a leftist utopia, where horrid things like racism and Rush Limbaugh don't exist. This is something you'd find in the redneck woods of Louisiana, not the cultured liberal paradise of the Golden State. It just bolstered the one theory I've had throughout my entire adult life that seems to be a constant no matter where I am . . . assholes are everywhere.

That was no comfort to me in that moment. My heart was broken, and my son's tears sliced open every old wound of racism I'd carried from my childhood. Suddenly it was me who was in elementary school—weeping, confused, wondering why my classmate called me a nigger, wondering why those boys on the school bus would tell me to go back to the cotton fields, wondering why I was so hated and so loathed. What had I done to deserve this pain?

I spent a lot of years, and a lot of prayers, learning the freedom of forgiveness, and it has been a theme in my life and in my work. Even still, I was helplessly transported back to being that lonely, helpless little girl; in that moment, I found myself defenseless against the rage.

We whispered some lame reassurances to our son, loved him up, and sent him on his way to play with his baby sister, who obviously was not nearly as cool and nearly as fun as Carrie. And then I turned to my husband and laid out a determined (and I thought, reasonable) plan.

"Okay," I began, "we're going over there. And I'm going to knock on the door and when he comes to the door, you're going to punch him in the face. And then I'm going to throw a brick through their window, key their car, and set it on fire."

I could only see red. I had not felt such rage since my childhood. It was one thing for me to be treated poorly by the people around me, but my son? My sweet, open, loving son whom everyone adored, who was the friend to every friendless child in his class, the little boy all the other moms would insist I "save" for their daughters to marry one day? My sweet baby? He'd never hurt a soul. He'd never even lived near White people before. He came from an exclusively Black neighborhood. He'd never known what it was like to be labeled as so "different" from his peers based solely on his skin. It wasn't anywhere in his frame of reference. His confusion was nearly as heartbreaking to me as his pain. It just wasn't fair.

But my husband—who is kind, and patient and practical and everything I am not—just looked at me and very calmly said,

"No. We're not going to do any of that. What we are going to do is extend to this family the same grace God extends to us."

Looking back now, it was advice that changed the trajectory of my life. At that moment, I did not appreciate it. I was not comforted. I was outraged. I had every right to be. I shouted at him. How dare he act so calm? Just what did that mean? What did he expect me to do? Invite them over for dinner? Go on a double date? Just how on earth am I supposed to show grace to the racists next door who just broke our son's heart?

I fumed and cried and fumed some more. I prayed for God to show me what "grace" looked like in this situation.

Here's the thing about grace: it isn't about being nice or kind or pretending an offense didn't happen. Grace means choosing not to treat someone the way you think they deserve to be treated. That is the "grace" my husband was admonishing me to bestow. We humans are fallen, sinful creatures. We default to poor behavior. We deserve punishment. God offers us salvation.

Grace.

I decided for me, in this situation, grace would simply mean me saying hello to my neighbors in the street, stopping for small talk at the mailbox, waving as they drove by. I did it, but it was hard. So very hard. Some days I would walk past the father and smile. My lips would be saying "hello," but my heart was screaming, "I hate you!" He seemed perplexed by my casual friendliness at first, but he always reciprocated the gestures.

The mother . . . she was a completely different situation. She steadily rebuffed my attempts at grace, and I struggled not to let it harden my heart. I didn't always win that battle. When I would see her driving past, I would wave. And she would pretend she didn't see me. When I saw her in the store I would smile and say hello. And she would look straight past me, as if I didn't exist. When I encountered her at the mailbox, I would ask her how she was doing. And she would turn her back and walk toward her home, as if I'd never said a word. She made me invisible which only increased my rage. But I persisted.

A few weeks after the incident, I walked outside to find my son and the neighbor girl playing together in the driveway, and they continued to play together, without intervention, every day after that. A year later, the mother drove past me, I raised my hand to offer her my usual, unwelcome wave . . . and she waved back.

We still know this family, although we are no longer neighbors. We're not best friends, but when I see the mother out and about, she calls me "neighbor," and we chat about the kids and the weather and rising cost of living. Our children are grown now, and when they are home for visits, they often briefly connect to catch up. They still consider each other the best of childhood friends.

My life was changed for the better by that encounter, and by the guiding grace of God (and fine, yes, some good advice from my husband, but don't tell him I admitted that). I learned a serious lesson about just how difficult it is to love when all you want to do is hate. I learned extinguishing the fires of hate in your own heart is a bigger challenge than demanding someone do it for themselves. I had wanted so badly to burn my neighbor's house down, quite literally. In this day and age, few people would have blamed me had I done it. But if I had burned down their house, I could have caught the entire neighborhood on fire. I could have destroyed us all.

This is how I instinctively knew CRT was never going to be a refining fire bringing peace and reconciliation. It could only be an uncontrolled blaze, started in rage, spread in our hearts, ending in mass destruction that catches the innocent in its smoky haze.

If all it was were a few lesson plans and some uncomfortable discussions, I could be on board for that. But this . . . this is something different. I want progress, but CRT is a regression. I don't think it's out of bounds to suggest Martin Luther King Jr. would roll over in his grave if he saw we'd voluntarily rolled ourselves all the way back to segregation after all that blood was spilled.

WHAT CAN YOU DO?

If there ever was a case of the squeaky wheel getting the grease, Critical Race Theory is it. The title itself is as empty as the concept. CRT is less of a "theory" and more of blank screen where one can project their grievances according to their mood. Blank screens are dangerous, because they are not rooted. They do not stand on a solid foundation. They can be manipulated to mean whatever it is the viewer wants them to mean. Conservative pundit Ben Shapiro likes to say, "Facts don't care about your feelings." Well, blank screens *only* care about your feelings, and feelings change quickly, particularly in the political landscape.

Robin DiAngelo's book *White Fragility* has become the most recent textbook for CRT. In it, DiAngelo lays out the CRT-supported theory that America is so steeped in racism that White Americans now completely lack the ability to acknowledge racial injustice. That inability renders them useless in the battle against racism. In fact, it renders them automatic enemies until they can prove otherwise. They are guilty simply by virtue of being White. If one rejects the assertion it is because they are too fragile to accept their part in the perpetuation of racism. If one accepts the assertion and makes attempts to become "anti-racist" they are most likely overcorrecting for their fragility. White "allies" are to be seen but not heard. A White person who wishes to stand up for Black people or defend against injustice is still using their White privilege to drown out Black voices, still making the assumption that what they say is what matters most. A White person who accepts the flawed logic of CRT yet continues to accept the "privilege" of whiteness is still a racist. A White person who admits they are a racist and seeks help or asks questions about how to become anti-racist is foisting their shortcomings upon minorities, who are already burdened by an inherently racist nation.

If you're wondering how White people win in this situation—they don't. That is another leg of the theory. White people need to stop "winning" and start being deliberate about losing—losing their privilege, their place, their voice, their entitlement. Interestingly (and unsurprisingly) the only White person who seems to get out from under this impossible dilemma in DiAngelo's book is DiAngelo herself. She wrote the book. Everyone else needs to step aside.

It would be funny if it weren't so destructive. CRT has been picked up by our mainstream media and their political allies and is now being used as a bludgeon to eliminate one side of the conversation. It is a constant stream of negativity and abuse toward a subsection of America based on their race. Hmmm . . . where have we heard this before?

"Equity" seeks to cut off the taller person at the knees, such that they are forced to match the height of those who are shorter. "Equality" gives everyone the same ladder and dares them to climb as high as they can.

There are no ladders in CRT.

CRT seeks to teach children shame for the way they were created. This was never okay to do to Black people and if anyone knows the lasting consequences of such strategy it is the Black community. I am beyond perplexed by why any of us would wish that upon anyone else. CRT does not seek to solve, but to blame and it's blaming all the wrong people.

We cannot thrive as a nation or as neighbors if we allow our children to grow up imagining each other as enemies rather than countrymen.

Conservatives—nay, just reasonable people in general, regardless of party—must draw the line here. Complaining is no longer enough. Those who have the means and the will need to start being the squeaky wheels, as distasteful as it sounds.

This is a very specific issue with very specific challenges, so at the risk of seeming a bit juvenile, I've compiled a strategies list in this instance. I think it's helpful to be able to check off some of these ideas if you can. Not every single point may be for you, but pick which one might be the area in which you draw your line and set up camp.

1. Exposure - using media to expose egregious lesson plans, assemblies, and lectures in our schools. Parents need to start documenting these things and posting them for friendly media to pick up and excoriate. The left uses this tactic to shame normality and it works. The right needs to do the same.

2. Ridicule - this is a popular and effective Alinsky principle. Ridiculing a notion creates shame around a notion. And this is a notion that deserves to be shamed.

3. Network - find other like-minded parents in your schools and form a group. Write letters, call

       legislators, complain at school board meetings.
       There is strength in numbers.

4. The law - hire lawyers to bring lawsuits against school districts that jam CRT curriculum through the system without parental approval or notification.

5. Power positions - run for school board, get on the parent/teacher board, run for council, make yourself a decision-maker. Government goes to those who show up.

As this book goes to publication, I am proud to say I have decided to draw my own lines in my own community. I'm taking my own advice. I am running for my school board. The decisions they have been making for our children over the last two years have been infuriating. I realize I've left the hard work to others for far too long. So, I'm throwing my hat in the ring. I'm drawing my lines. Pick your metaphor. I hope by the time you have this book in your hands I can tell you I am an elected member of my district's school board.

CHAPTER 8

CIVIL RIGHTS AND COVID FIGHTS

I've hesitated to write this chapter. In fact, it is the last chapter I've tackled in this tome. That's because the story of COVID, as I write, has not in itself finished being written. So much is changing day-to-day, state-to-state, it feels impossible to offer specific advice about this phenomenon.

Suffice to say, this global pandemic has brought this nation to places we couldn't have imagined. Conservatives, and libertarians especially, have always had a myriad of complaints about government overreach and the waning sanctity of the Constitution. There has always been a tension between individual rights and our responsibilities to each other as a society. Our Founding Fathers did their best to protect us from each other and from the threat of an oppressive government. Being the initiators of a revolution, the harsh reality of living under an uncaring and distant bureaucracy with no right to object to their rule embedded in them a sense of urgency to secure the God-given rights of the citizens of this burgeoning nation.

There are many who argue we should not hallow this great document because when it was formed it was not formed for everyone. We were still embroiled in the sin of slavery. John

Adams felt it was the greatest failure of his life that he was not
able to successfully advocate for the abolishment of slavery to
be included in this new, experimental charter. It was a failure
causing great tension between Adams and his wife, Abigail,
who was a passionate abolitionist.

I find that fact comforting, because it means although
flawed men excluded the personhood of victims of the slave
trade, the notion was not completely absent from our founding.
It was present and palpable, and the Founding Fathers did a
very clever thing: they made the language broad—*all men*—and
they left mechanisms within the Constitution to eventually
make changes as our sense of humanity evolved.

They also purposefully left the administration of human
rights to the Creator of human rights. This assured no man
could be the arbiter of our rights, because no man—not the
king, not the president—is higher or mightier than God Himself. It left the door open for good men and women to eventually mount legal and moral challenges to the institution of
slavery, and to finally get us to a place where our Constitution
was allowed to embrace all it was originally intended to. We
eventually got there. We spent too long getting there, but the
overwhelming spirit of freedom with which our country was
founded could not be contained by the evils of slavery and
segregation. Our fight to secure our civil rights as Americans
was not a fight to invent those rights, but to restore them.

I say all this because I believe our current battles to sustain
our civil rights in the face of an overbearing government that
wants to restrict them in the name of "public health" is a direct
result of our slow but steady journey away from the most fundamental aspect of the Constitution of the United States of
America.

That is, that there is a God and He and He alone bestows
our rights, and furthermore, He cares for us and protects us.

John Adams left us with this corroborating thought:

> Our Constitution was made only for a moral and religious
> people. It is wholly inadequate to the government of
> any other.[1]

Our progressive friends and opponents have worked hard for decades to shift us away from a national dependence on God. He has been pushed from the public square in the name of "equity." The establishment clause—meant to protect against the formation of a state church—has been used to clobber religious Americans and beat back the shared spirit of creation by a Creator. If we cannot agree on the very basic idea our rights come from someone or something higher than man, then we cannot effectively administer our Constitution. It rests on the very shoulders of God.

Space abhors a vacuum, and the Word tells us humans are born with a God-shaped hole in our hearts. If it's not filled with God, it will be filled with a god. We find ourselves currently in a situation where too many Americans have filled that hole in our hearts with the god of Big Government.

When COVID appeared, we were all terrified of the unknown. The unprecedented step to shut people off from their daily lives and close their businesses and schools could only happen if we as a people, generally speaking, do not act as though our rights derive from God alone. We allowed the government to usurp those rights in the name of public safety and it's been a hellish battle since to regain them inch by inch.

I, like so many others, believed the lie of "fifteen days to slow the spread." I wanted to do my part as we faced off against a terrifying new threat that could not be repelled by weapons or armies. Our mainstream media, utterly devoid of curiosity by this point (as we have previously discussed in this book) took the opportunity to make the virus political, and it has been a nightmare ever since. When someone asks you why a virus has been made so political by so many people, remind them our media and Donald Trump's political opponents made it so from the very start.

When Trump announced Operation Warp Speed—the lifting of the bureaucratic red tape to allow companies to be able to fast-track COVID vaccine research and development— the progressive left screamed bloody murder. They would never trust a vaccine made at the hands of the most racist, evil, tyrannical president since the last most racist, evil tyrannical president (they are always Republicans, coincidentally). When Trump released federal Navy hospital ships to take up port in supposedly overwhelmed cities like San Francisco and New York City, they were turned away by those Democrat governors. They wouldn't accept help from the Worst President Ever™ even if that help could save lives.

The progressives like to tell us it is those alt-right, toothless, redneck, idiot conservatives who have politicized masks. They forget (or choose to forget) it was conservatives who said masks should be an individual choice, not mandated. We were all for their use if that's what a person felt was the right thing to do. That's hardly a tyrannical point of view and it wasn't even a rebuke of masks, it was simply an affirmation of freedom. The progressives wouldn't even accept a compromise. On liberal outlets and on social media, progressives declared anyone who refused to don a mask cold-hearted, ignorant, murderous, and granny-killers. Then they wondered and still to this day wonder why people have dug in their heels on mask mandates and feel suspicious of anyone demanding they wear one when they don't prefer to.

They made it political, because they have made government their god and god has spoken. Mask up or go to hell. And ironically, once President Trump was no longer in office, they took to the vaccines like pigs in experimental manure. Get your vaccine or go to hell.

Their god was government. Their patron saint of health was Doctor Fauci. Their angels were nurses. Their rosaries were masks. Their church was a Zoom screen.

There are no worse religious zealots than political religious zealots. If conservatives had their way, none of this would be political and it would only be about choice. But choice is dangerous, because people choose wrong. Underneath the fear and the devotion to Big Government is the unchecked desire to control one's surroundings by controlling everyone and everything in it. There is a belief if we can just enact enough laws, punish enough people, we can condition people to make the "right" choices, and we can create paradise.

This is why John Adams explained that our Constitution is one for a religious—read: churched—people. Only a moral and religious population can understand and even welcome the concept of a loving Creator being in control. There is a peace that comes with knowing our free will is perverted by original sin, and the gaps that sin leaves are covered by an Almighty God who ultimately holds the fate of both the entire universe and smallest individual in His hands. We don't have to bind the will of the people to force a desired outcome. We pray and trust even in the midst of suffering God has a plan.

It is a bridge too far for many on the left. If God is in control, they are not, and there is a certain type of person who is enraged by the thought. In fact, that was the original sin. The primary sin of Adam and Eve wasn't they ate something they weren't supposed to or listened to someone they weren't supposed to listen to. It wasn't that Eve "tricked" her husband into disobeying God, or that Adam led them both into disobedience. Their primary sin was wanting to *be* God. The serpent told them God was keeping something from them—the one thing that could make them happy and powerful, the one thing would make them like Him.

Perhaps you weren't expecting me to close out this book by taking it to church, as I like to say on my podcast. But I am a Christian. I believe firmly in a God who directs our steps. I believe this nation has been made great for such a time of this, and specifically because of our foundational beliefs in the Almighty Creator.

So whether we're talking about transgender issues, or the battle over education or COVID mandates or cancel culture, what we are always really talking about is the human impulse to reject God, and make ourselves god. It is rebellion. This is all rebellion.

I've always said the "gospel of freedom" and the gospel of Christ go hand-in-hand. They are one in the same, even if I use one as a political reference and one as a religious reference. When you understand you can't control every circumstance around you, you are gifted a freedom which allows you to assess and accept risk.

The harshness of the COVID response from around the world is the result of the grossly perverted mindset that we can reach perfection if we can just control human nature. That is the same lie telling us we can do God's job better than He can. The very heart of freedom is choice. Just like God's original plan. If you can't choose to love, is it really love? If our government restrains our choice, it is in effect restraining our freedom.

CHAPTER 9

ARE WE WAKING UP TOO LATE?

I realize there are a lot of people out there, maybe even you, who think perhaps the scales have tipped too far. I'm not suggesting there is a rose petal path to success here, but when I talk to my left-wing friends, I hear them saying things we are. They feel they are losing ground; they feel their representatives aren't being bold enough; they feel the media isn't doing their jobs properly and it is reflecting poorly on liberal America. Admittedly, we might look at their complaints and scoff, for we, too, feel we are on the losing end of things.

I find a bit of comfort in it all. We will always imagine our "side" to be the underdog, to be struggling, to be unheard. That's human nature. If our ideological opponents are feeling like they're losing—whether it's true or not—it indicates there is still plenty of room to maneuver. There is always more work to do, more steps to take, more paths to break. When we stop believing that, then we can tell ourselves it's time to pack it in. I'm not there yet. I hope this book helps you realize you aren't either.

BUT WE'VE NEVER BEEN MORE DIVIDED

All the way back to the founding of this nation, when we were not yet a nation but a collection of tiny nations, countrymen held each other in quite a bit of contempt. George Washington was a great leader, but he was also an arrogant man, and found himself repulsed by many of the ragtag soldiers from other colonies. He felt they were crude, uncivilized, unkempt, and intellectually stunted. He thought about leaving his post on more than one occasion.

The men who fought under him felt the same about each other. Often fights would break out in the camps. Washington had to work to keep some factions separate in order to avoid war breaking out in their own circles. Sometimes men would simply get up and walk away from the camps, deciding they'd had enough and anxious to get home to tend to their families and crops.

At times there was little loyalty, little cooperation, and as much animus toward each other was toward the British. They were rarely of one mind. They tired often. They complained. They felt helpless and hopeless.

We think of our revolutionary forefathers as exclusively brave and courageous men and women, and while bravery certainly played a part, the truth is closer to what we see today. They were divided.

We have always been divided, on everything from slavery to women's rights to which coast is the best coast. We lost 600,000 American souls on the back of division. Perhaps it is a bit of modern arrogance to suppose we wouldn't be just as bitterly divided to this day. It is in our national genetics.

It is important to remember the goal here is not national unity. How naive of us to believe such a thing could ever happen. When has it ever happened? No, our goal is not to demand unity or fight for unity. We don't need unity. Somehow our country has made it this far without it. Our goal, instead, should be to drag the other side to tolerance. That is all we are demanding from our left-wing counterparts. Tolerance. If we can learn to tolerate the presence and opinion of one another then we can consider that a victory. Tolerance can push back the creeping incursion of corporate America into shaping state law. Tolerance can protect our young women from damaging social movements. Tolerance can push back extremism by giving bad ideas space to breathe and then be soundly refuted. Tolerance can soften the blade of division, at least enough for us to allow each other to live our own lives without thrusting our preferences upon those around us. Tolerance will be how we protect our future. Unity is a childish concept and why would we want to unify with people whose fundamental belief systems are so drastically different from our own? If we can convince our opposition to finally accept a philosophy of true tolerance, we can leave the big decisions to the ballot box, the way it was always meant to be. There is peace in that. I'm not saying it's possible, I'm just saying we have a duty to fight for it.

As you move ahead, as you decide where your own line is and how you will draw it, remember our ultimate goal is not vengeance but tolerance. Do not abandon grace—and in all things remember the grace that was given to you, to me, to all of us as a nation. Grace is always the best strategy, but grace does not preclude action. Now is the time for us to stand up corporately and demand to be seen, demand our Constitution be respected, and demand our politicians represent us and not corporations or the grievance industry or anything else attempting to subvert the will of the people.

Make your call. Stake out your ground. Draw your line in the sand and then stand there and do not move. For one person, it may be an impossible task. For all of us together, it could be a thrilling victory.

ONE SMALL RIPPLE, MANY WAVES

You know the saying . . . every little bit counts. That applies here as much as anywhere. I think a big reason why conservatives will often hang back from the public square is they feel like nothing they can offer will make a difference. How will running for the Board of Directors for your local library make any difference at all when it comes to the massive social disruptions we are currently living through?

Here's the thing: you're not saving America and you can't and won't do that on your own. That's a heavy burden. Take it off your shoulders. You're just a drop in the bucket of time, in this current moment, but a drop makes a ripple, and a ripple is all it takes to change everything. We are all walking ripples, if you think about it. Our very existences change the direction of history. What if you added a bit of spice to that ripple? Run for that position at the library. Who knows what ripples you can make or who you could inspire? I know this: you being in that position is far better than someone who wants to turn the library into an Antifa autonomous zone.

Let me end with something very non-political here. A short story about a man who wasn't supposed to be. A story about a "mistake" which left one person alive, and then created many persons and many stories and much beauty.

This story is about my father-in-law, whom I have mentioned in this book. He was his mother's favorite child, the golden child, but it wasn't until later in his life he found out his mother had once attempted to abort him. She was poor and Black and single in 1950s Michigan, and the mother of seven children. Her options were limited and the dread surely must have been overwhelming. We can't blame her making a desperate choice in desperate times, but we can thank God her choice was thwarted by a bigger plan. My father-in-law was born anyway, just another Black boy in segregated America.

That Black boy went on—through struggles and trials—to become a man, a father, a husband, a pastor. He dedicated his life to serving others, and I promise you I could fill an arena with people who have a story to tell about how influential Victor Davis has been in their lives. I often think about all of the ripple effects of his life, and how random but influential they have been. I would not even be writing this book, from this state, and this home, with these people if his mother's original choice had been successful. If anything you've read in this book has had any kind of positive effect, you can count yourself as a part of that one small ripple.

I asked my father-in-law to briefly share with me how he has seen the ripples of his life play out. That's no small task for him. Part of his story is a tale of grief, having lost two sons at the same time in the prime of their lives. Those ripples aren't always sent out into calm waters. Rather than retell what he had to say, I'll simply share it with you directly:

> Reflecting on how the experiences of our lives, like drops striking the water impacts shorelines beyond our ability to comprehend.
>
> While we began in separate circumstances, Faith's birth nearly resulted in her mother's death, and as a result her mom named her "Faith." My mother successfully aborted a male child only to shortly thereafter find herself pregnant with me and being so despondent, she attempted to abort me. However somehow, I was able to be born and she named me "Victor."
>
> Years later, as teenagers we met and fell in love, marrying at the tender ages of 16 and 19. Being young and foolish, we managed to hurt and wound one another and even separated for a brief period. However, there were powers at work in our lives we were unaware of, directing and guiding us to fight for our covenant relationship.
>
> We repaired our relationship and marriage and went on to have three sons and a daughter, and during this process we gave our lives to Christ and surrendered to the point where I felt the call to the ministry of the gospel.
>
> Because of our early experience of nearly allowing our marriage to become another "black failed statistic," Faith and I felt called to give ourselves to strengthening other struggling couples. This resulted in numerous marriages, individuals, and households

being saved, with generational impact that is still being realized even today.

Another example of the "ripple effect" was seen as we tragically lost our two oldest sons in an automobile accident. Michael and Scott were thirty and twenty-five years, both married with lovely wives and five children between them. As painful as the experience was, my wife and I can look back and see how the Lord used this incident to radically change us from being a single family (focused on ourselves and our plans and desires) to see the enormity and significance of the family of God and the family of believers. So many people from all walks of life helped us "eat the elephant" of hurt and pain we found ourselves facing. Each one took an appropriate "bite" of our all-encompassing grief and left us with just enough for us to live through. Thus this "tragedy" not only impacted and shaped our lives, but also changed (and continues to change) the lives of others every time they face difficulty or share our "loss" with others.

Faith and Victor Davis have four children, eleven grandchildren, and (so far) sixteen great-grandchildren. They will have children and their children will have children and their grandchildren will have children . . . on and on. Which one of them will become a leader, a great artist, an inventor? Which one will find the cure for the incurable? Which one will be the person who will save or love the one who will find the cure for the incurable? We have no way to see beyond this moment in time, but we have so much proof even the smallest actions among us can reverberate beyond what our mortal minds can imagine. That thing you've been holding back from—perhaps because you are too scared or perhaps because you think it's pointless—do it anyway. Throw the pebble. Draw the line.

One small act can ripple throughout the ages . . . but what if you decided to make a wave?

NOTES

Chapter 1: Women's Rights and the Transgender Movement

1. Marni Sommer, Virginia Kamowa, Therese Mahon, "Opinion: Creating a more equal post-COVID-19 world for people who menstruate," DevEx, May 28, 2020, https://www.devex.com/news/sponsored/opinion-creating-a-more-equal-post-covid-19-world-for-people-who-menstruate-97312#.XtwLnv0aEeR.twitter.

2. Abby Gardner, "A Complete Breakdown of the J.K. Rowling Transgender-Comments Controversy," *Glamour*, July 20, 2021, https://www.glamour.com/story/a-complete-breakdown-of-the-jk-rowling-transgender-comments-controversy.

3. Mary Margaret Olohan, "Exclusive: California Forces Transgender 'Belief System' on Female Prisoners Housed with Biological Males, Lawsuit Says," *Daily Signal*, November 17, 2021, https://www.dailysignal.com/2021/11/17/exclusive-california-forces-transgender-belief-system-on-female-prisoners-housed-with-biological-males-lawsuit-says/.

4. Mark Lungariello, "Virginia board member resigns amid handling of sex assault claims," *New York Post*, October 15, 2021, https://nypost.com/2021/10/15/virginia-board-member-resigns-amid-handling-of-sex-assault-claim/.

5. Sam Dorman, "Virginia teacher placed on leave after speech disputing 'biological boy can be a girl and vice versa,'" Fox News, May 28, 2021, https://www.foxnews.com/us/virginia-teacher-leave-gender-speech.

Chapter 2: School Choice

1. "Systemic racism," Cambridge.org, https://dictionary.cambridge .org/us/dictionary/english/systemic-racism.

2. "Average Public School Spending/Student," Publicschoolreview .com, (2021–22), https://www.publicschoolreview.com/average-spending-student-stats/national-data#google_vignette.

3. Lou Adler, "New Survey Reveals 85% of All Jobs are Filled Via Networking," Linkedin survey, February 29, 2016, https://www .linkedin.com/pulse/new-survey-reveals-85-all-jobs-filled-via-networking-lou-adler.

4. Tyler Kingkade, "In wealthy Loudoun County, Virginia, parents face threats in battle over equity in schools," June 1, 2021, https:// www.nbcnews.com/news/us-news/wealthy-loudoun-county-virginia-parents-face-threats-battle-over-equity-n1269162.

5. Jon Levine, "Powerful teachers union influenced CDC on school reopenings, emails show", The New York Post, May 1, 2021 https:// nypost.com/2021/05/01/teachers-union-collaborated-with-cdc-on-school-reopening-emails/

6. Supreme Court of the United States, JANUS v. AMERICAN FEDERATION OF STATE, COUNTY, AND MUNICIPAL EMPLOYEES, COUNCIL 31, ET AL, June 27, 2018, https:// www.supremecourt.gov/opinions/17pdf/16-1466_2b3j.pdf

Chapter 3: Cancel Culture

1. David H. Weaver, Lars Willnat, G. Cleveland Wilhoit, "The American Journalist in the Digital Age: Another Look at U.S. News People," *Journalism and Mass Communication Quarterly* 96, no. 1 (March 2019): 101–30, https://journals.sagepub.com/doi/10.1177 /1077699018778242#_i1.

2. Aaron Calvin, "Meet Carson King, the 'Iowa Legend' who's raised more than $1 million for charity off of a sign asking for beer money," September 24, 2019, https://www.desmoinesregister.com/story/ sports/college/iowa-state/football/2019/09/24/meet-carson-king-whos-raised-over-1-million-charity-asking-beer-money-childrens-hospital-tweet/2427538001/.

3. Carol Hunter, "Register editor: Here's how we reported on Carson King's tweets," September 25, 2019, https://www.desmoinesregister .com/story/news/2019/09/24/carson-king-des-moines-register-how-reported-tweets-iowa-state-gameday-busch-venmo-children-hospital/2437436001/.

4. Saul Alinsky, *Rules for Radicals* (New York: Vintage Books, 1971), 130.

5. Anneta Konstantinides, "'Bachelor' host Chris Harrison apologizes for 'perpetuating racism' after defending controversial contestant," February 11, 2021, https://news.yahoo.com/bachelor-host-chris-harrison-apologizes-191528427.html.

6. *Totally Biased with W. Kamau Bell*, Comedy Central, 2016, https:// youtu.be/up1qyxHSbCg?t=108

7. "Gina Carano fired from 'Mandalorian' after social media post," Associated Press via PBS, February 11, 2021, https://www.pbs.org/ newshour/arts/gina-carano-fired-from-mandalorian-after-social-media-post.

Chapter 4: Corporate Oppression

1. Kira Davis, *Just Listen to Yourself* podcast, 2021, episodes 75–76, 99,101, https://open.spotify.com/show/02zQxBYuv7bHZt4X FTkyJN.

2. Faith Karimi, "It's now illegal in Georgia to give food and water to voters in line," CNN, March 26, 2021, https://www.cnn .com/2021/03/26/politics/georgia-voting-law-food-drink-ban-trnd/ index.html.

3. Kira Davis, "Woke Capitalism with Jeff Webb," *Just Listen to Yourself*, 2021, episodes 106, 108, https://open.spotify.com/ show/02zQxBYuv7bHZt4XFTkyJN.

Chapter 5: Big Tech, Big Media, Big Problems

1. "I would tell you how many followers I lost but I have no idea what I had before because I'm an adult," Twitter, @JakeTapper, January 10, 2021, https://twitter.com/jaketapper/status/134835 2082529710080.

2. "Anti-vaxxer," Merriam-Webster.com, *Merriam-Webster Dictionary*, https://www.merriam-webster.com/dictionary/anti-vaxxer.

3. "Anti-vaxxer," Dictionary.com, https://www.dictionary.com/browse/antivax.

4. Frieda Powers, "Anyone less self-aware? Brian Stelter frets over partisan 'echo chambers' with rise of conservative media," BizPac Review, November 13, 2020, https://www.bizpacreview.com/2020/11/13/anyone-less-self-aware-brian-stelter-frets-over-partisan-echo-chambers-with-rise-of-conservative-media-996116/

Chapter 6: Rewriting History

1. James Cary, "1984 and All That Hideous Strength," Substack, November 26, 2021, https://jamescary.substack.com/p/1984-and-all-that-hideous-strength.

Chapter 7: Critical Race Theory (Here Goes Nothin')

1. Tom Jones, "Parent files complaint against Atlanta elementary school, alleges it's segregating classes," WSB-TV, August 08, 2021, https://www.wsbtv.com/news/local/parent-files-complaint-against-atlanta-elementary-school-alleges-its-segregating-classes/2PNTBQDPQRCM7CXJTESRXUTMJE/.

2. "A Pathway to Equitable Math Instruction: Dismantling racism in mathematics instruction," front page, equitablemath.org.

3. "A Pathway to Equitable Math Instruction," page 6, https://equitablemath.org/wp-content/uploads/sites/2/2020/11/1_STRIDE1.pdf

Chapter 8: Civil Rights and COVID Fights

1. Letter from John Adams to Massachusetts Militia (October 11, 1798), https://founders.archives.gov/documents/Adams/99-02-02-3102.

Just Listen to Yourself with Kira Davis is a podcast that breaks down the talking points of hot topics and ideas and draws them all the way out to their logical conclusions.

With humor and relatability, Kira challenges listeners to examine their beliefs and dig into what they're really saying when they espouse those beliefs. This award-winning show is available wherever you find your podcasts.

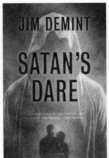
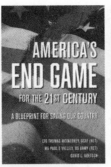

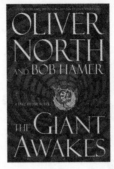

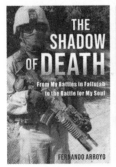